The Middle Ages

The Middle Ages

Trevor Cairns

Published in cooperation with Cambridge University Press
Lerner Publications Company, Minneapolis

LIBRARY OF CONGRESS CATALOGING IN PUBLICATION DATA

Cairns, Trevor.
The Middle Ages.

(Cambridge Introduction to History, v. 4)
SUMMARY: Considers the most important aspects of
European history between 1000 and 1450, including the power
of the guilds, the Church, the feudal lords, and the Crusades.

1. Civilization, Medieval—Juvenile literature. [1. Civilization, Medieval. 2. Middle Ages] I. Title.

CB351.C23 1974   914′.03′1   74-10976
ISBN 0-8225-0804-4

This edition first published 1975 by Lerner Publications Company
by permission of Cambridge University Press.

Copyright © MCMLXXII by Cambridge University Press.
Original edition published as part of *The Cambridge Introduction to the History of Mankind.*

International Standard Book Number: 0-8225-0804-4
Library of Congress Catalog Card Number: 74-10976

Manufactured in the United States of America.

This edition is available exclusively from:
Lerner Publications Company, 241 First Avenue North, Minneapolis, Minnesota 55401

3   4   5   6   7   8   9   10   85   84   83   82

Contents

List of Maps and Diagrams

Editors' Note

In preparing this edition of *The Cambridge Introduction to History* for publication, the editors have made only a few minor changes in the original material. In some isolated cases, British spelling and usage were altered in order to avoid possible confusion for our readers. Whenever necessary, information was added to clarify references to people, places, and events in British history. An index and a list of maps and diagrams were also provided in each volume.

THE CHURCH — those who pray.
Drawing of an archbishop from the Lambeth Apocalypse,
written in England in the thirteenth century.

THE FEUDAL LORDS — those who fight.
Drawing from the Holkham Bible, written in England
in the fourteenth century.

THE ORDINARY PEOPLE — those who work.
Painting from the Bedford Book of Hours, a prayer book
written in France in the fifteenth century.

This book is about a period of history called THE MIDDLE AGES. The name is a poor one, for it tells us nothing at all about the people who lived then, or about what happened. The obvious question is: 'Middle of what?'

The answer is: 'Between ancient history and modern history.'

The idea used to be this:

ANCIENT   Greek   Roman

People in Europe were civilised in the time of the Greeks and Romans

People in Europe were less civilised during the thousand years in between – the MIDDLE AGES

MODERN   16th   17th   18th   19th   20th   centuries

People in Europe have been civilised since about 1450

As you see, the name suggests that those thousand years were no more than a long interval, when nothing worthwhile was going on. The early part is sometimes even called 'The Dark Ages'. Since you already know something about that part, which was the period of the barbarian invasions, of the spread of Christianity and Islam, of the Viking raids, of such men as St Benedict, the Emperor Justinian, Charles the Great and King Alfred, you can decide whether or not 'Dark Ages' is a good name. The real Middle Ages are the centuries from about 1000 to about 1450.

It would be strange if nothing very interesting happened in Europe during all this time. In fact there were two very important things about the way people lived together – or, to use a better phrase, the way society was organised – during the Middle Ages.

First, the CHURCH. Everyone in western Europe believed in the same Church, and this made it very powerful. It tried to see that everyone did as it commanded, because the Church alone knew what God wanted; or so people thought.

Second, the FEUDAL LORDS. These were the warrior noblemen who wore armour, rode horses and lived in castles. They were the ruling class all over Europe during the Middle Ages. They obeyed the king of their country when they wanted to, and they looked down on the ordinary people as being altogether lower creatures than themselves.

While the Church and the feudal lords kept their grip, the Middle Ages went on. When the Church and the lords found power slipping out of their grasp more and more into the hands of the merchants and the kings, the Middle Ages came to an end.

So we could call these centuries 'The Age of Church and Lords': but it is rather a mouthful, and everyone knows the old name already. There is a well-known adjective, too: 'medieval', from the Latin for 'Middle Ages'. Therefore, as long as we remember the ideas which lie behind it, it is more convenient to go on using the name that everyone recognises.

1. The Church

The parish priest

THE CHURCH BUILDINGS. If you live in England, you are sure to be fairly near an old parish church. Sometimes it may be Anglo-Saxon, but usually it will date from some time between about 1000 and 1500. You ought to be able to tell how old it is by looking at it, because builders changed their styles during the Middle Ages, beginning with massive, solid work and making buildings lighter and more delicate-looking as the centuries went on and the builders became more skilful.

Sometimes you may find a church like this one at Iffley. The style of building is called Romanesque. If you think of how the Romans had built, especially their rounded arches, you will understand why. In England this style is often called 'Norman', because so much was done in the century or so after 1066 by Norman kings, bishops and lords. In these buildings you may often find rows of patterns carved round the tops of doors and windows, especially a zigzag or 'chevron' pattern.

Frequently, though, your church will have doors and windows arched very differently, pointed like these at Grantham. The pointed arch was one of the great inventions of medieval builders. As time went on they made their buildings altogether more pointed, and often added tall spires to the towers. This style of architecture is called 'Gothic' – a stupid name, because it was certainly not the work of the Goths, whom you may remember long before, in the barbarian invasions. The name Gothic was invented by sixteenth-century people who thought that because this style was not like the architecture of the Greeks and Romans it was uncivilised, barbarous; so they called it Gothic, just as we call barbarous, destructive people 'Vandals'. Though nowadays it has lost its original meaning, the name 'Gothic' has remained because, just as with the name 'Middle Ages', everybody has got used to it.

Heavy round arches and pillars in a Norman church: Melbourne, Derbyshire.

Thirteenth-century Gothic pointed arches and clustered pillars: Grantham, Lincolnshire.

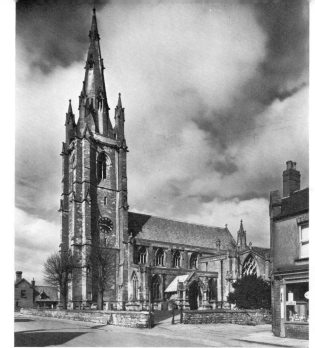

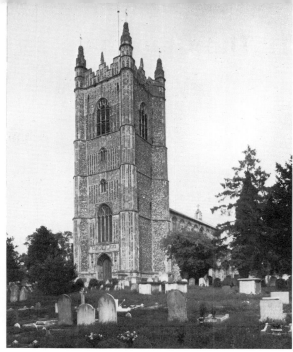

left: A twelfth-century Norman church: Iffley, Oxfordshire, seen from the west.

right: Fourteenth-century Decorated Gothic: Heckington, Lincolnshire, from the south.
far right: The fifteenth-century Perpendicular style: Redenhall, Norfolk, from the west.

As time went on, Gothic architecture became more delicate and ornamented. Towards the end of the Middle Ages it grew into its lightest and most daring form in England, with lofty flattened arches and enormously wide windows. You can see why this style has been named 'Perpendicular'. Many churches in the Perpendicular style were built by rich wool merchants both in East Anglia and in the west of England during the fifteenth century.

Often you will find churches which kept on being enlarged and altered during the Middle Ages, so that they are part Romanesque, part Gothic, part Decorated Gothic, and in England may be part Perpendicular as well.

Whatever the style of building, every village had at least one small church, normally with a priest. A town often had a big church, with several priests, and as a town grew more churches would have to be built, each with its priest to look after the people in the parish. More people, though, lived in villages.

left: The nearly flat arches inside a Perpendicular church: Chipping Camden, Gloucestershire.

7

The replica rood screen dominates the great church at Saffron Walden, Essex, as the original must have done in the fifteenth century. *below:* Drawing of a twelfth-century Last Judgment painted on the church wall at Chaldon, Surrey (the original is now very faded).

INSIDE THE CHURCH. Everybody went to church on Sundays and on other holy-days, such as the feasts of important saints. The Church ordered that these days should be kept for the worship of God, free from ordinary everyday work. These were the only days off that people had, and we still use the same word, holiday. People came to church to attend Mass, as the main morning service was called, and sometimes the priest would preach, telling them of God and the saints, and urging them to lead good lives.

Few, if any, of the people in a parish church would be able to read, and in any case there would be no prayer books for them. All books were very expensive. The priest's sermon would be in ordinary language, but the Mass would be in Latin, the language which the Church used in every country. Probably most people were so used to it that they could tell what was going on, even if they could not understand the words; but in case their eyes and minds began to wander from what the priest was doing, the inside of the church would contain pictures and statues for them to look at, to make them think about religious matters.

Most of these pictures and statues have been destroyed, and the few which have survived were mostly made in the later part of the Middle Ages. Still there remain enough for us to be able to imagine what the inside of a church was like then. Looking forward, a worshipper would see a screen in front of the altar, often beautifully carved and with the panels painted. On top of this screen there would be a rood, or big crucifix, so that nobody could forget how and why Christ had died. On the walls, and sometimes over the arch above the rood, were paintings. One popular subject was the Last Judgment, showing the dead rising from their graves and being judged, the good being taken up to live with God in Heaven, and the bad being sent to suffer torture for ever in Hell.

Sometimes the whole inside of the church would be covered by paintings. Here is an Italian church with walls still covered by masterpieces painted in the early fourteenth century. In England there is nothing as good as this, but some churches now have wall-paintings which have been discovered quite recently after being whitewashed over for hundreds of years.

right: The interior of the Scrovegni Chapel, Padua, is covered with scenes from the life of Christ, painted soon after 1300 by the great Italian artist Giotto.

CHURCH AND PEOPLE. The parish church was usually the finest building in the village, often the only stone one. Even today, as this photograph illustrates, the church often dominates a village or small town. Nobody could forget it. Every Sunday and holy-day the people went there. The parish priest christened them, married them, visited them when they were ill, and buried them. He tried to make them friends of God; without the Church they would have no chance of going to Heaven. Even in the business of this world, the priest would often be needed to give his help and advice, for there would usually be no other man in the village with any sort of education.

The people of the parish did not get all this for nothing. The priest had to eat and to have a house. The church, like any big building, needed constant looking after. Perhaps any expensive work on the church, or the presentation of precious vessels to be used on the altar, would be paid for by some very rich man – a lord or, towards the end of the Middle Ages, a merchant. All the same, the ordinary peasants would pay tithes (a tenth of their income) and make special offerings at times like Easter. Also, all believed that it was good to give to the poor or to the Church or the Crusade; generous people would be rewarded by God in Heaven.

The bishop

The priest was a very important man in his own parish, but this did not mean that he had the right to do exactly as he pleased. He had to obey the bishop. The bishop's task was to look after parish priests, to see that they behaved well and to appoint new ones.

The map shows how England was divided into bishoprics. Inside each bishopric, or diocese, the bishop ruled over all the priests and most of the monks and nuns who lived there. You can see that a bishop held great power.

At Norwich the Norman bishop's throne stands in what had been the traditional place for a 'cathedra' since the time of Roman basilicas: at the far end, behind even the high altar.

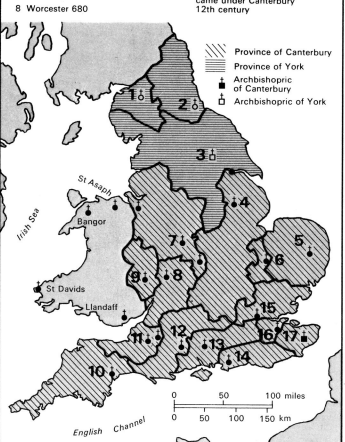

Medieval bishoprics and archbishoprics of England and Wales

1　Carlisle 1133
2　Durham, trs. first from Lindisfarne, then from Chester-le-Street 995
3　York 625
4　Lincoln trs. from Dorchester 1072
5　Norwich, trs. first from Elmham, then from Thetford 1091
6　Ely 1109
7　Lichfield 669 after 1100 sometimes also at Coventry and Chester
8　Worcester 680
9　Hereford 676
10　Exeter trs. from Crediton 1050
11　Bath and Wells 909
12　Salisbury trs. from Sherborne 1078
13　Winchester 662
14　Chichester trs. from Selsey 1075
15　London 604
16　Rochester 604
17　Canterbury 597

unless a transfer is indicated, dates given are those of the foundation of the see
Welsh bishoprics fd. 6th century; came under Canterbury 12th century

⧄⧄⧄ Province of Canterbury
═══ Province of York
✚ Archbishopric of Canterbury
▢ Archbishopric of York

St Asaph
Bangor
Irish Sea
St Davids
Llandaff

0   50   100 miles
0   50   100   150 km

English Channel

If a priest was accused of committing a crime, he was not tried in an ordinary court, by the lord of the manor or by the king's judges. Only a churchman could judge a churchman, so the bishop held a court for such cases. This court also tried men who were not priests if they were accused of offences against the Church, or if they were involved in a dispute over marriage or over wills – for, as you know, the Church married and buried everyone. There was so much work for the bishop's court that he handed it over to the archdeacon, and there were many lawyers who made a special study of Church Law, or Canon Law as it was called, and worked only in Church courts.

Such important churchmen as bishops were expected to keep up a dignified state. In his main church each bishop had a throne, where he sat during some services. The Latin word for a throne is 'cathedra', and so the chief church of a bishopric is known as a cathedral.

At Durham the Decorated Gothic throne, said to be the highest in Christendom, stands in what has become the normal place: before and to one side of the high altar. The bishop who built it lies proudly below.

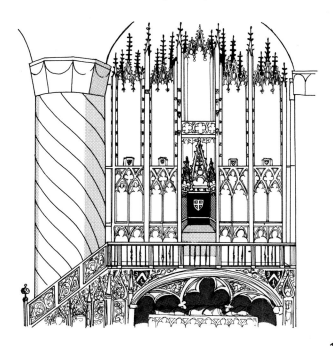

At Albi, in southern France, once the centre of the Albigensian heresy, the cathedral towers fortress-like over the city.

The cathedral, the mother church of the whole diocese, naturally had to be as splendid as possible. There must be space for multitudes to worship, for large choirs, for elaborate processions. There must be a high altar for the main services, and smaller altars in side chapels, where people could have private services if they wished. There would be a specially holy place where the relics of a saint were kept, or perhaps some venerated statue, and it had to be so arranged that pilgrims could come to visit this shrine. Outside, it was fitting that the cathedral should be of equal magnificence, with soaring towers and rich carving to remind people both far and near of the majesty of God and His Church.

Often there were other buildings beside the cathedral. Sometimes a wall, with gates, was built to form a 'close' round the cathedral. The bishop would need a house near the cathedral. Such a great church required many priests, or 'canons', to conduct services, and they also needed somewhere convenient to live.

There are so many great medieval cathedrals, in so many different styles of building, each with its own particular splendours, that it is only possible here to show enough to suggest the rich variety. Look at the pictures on the next two pages, and think about the purpose of each of the things you see.

Think also of the amount of labour, skill, time and treasure which must have gone into the cathedral.

And notice how we have been able to take examples from all over western Europe – Medieval Western Christendom.

left: The west end of a cathedral is usually a very impressive setting for the main entrance: Frombork, Poland.

below left: Entering, the worshipper looks straight up the nave towards the high altar: Cefalu, Sicily.

below: Behind the high altar, the chief centre of worship, the reredos, or screen, gleams in splendour: Gerona, Spain.

left:
Before the
high altar is
the choir,
sometimes
enclosed and
furnished
with
elaborately
carved stalls
for the
clergy:
Norwich,
England.

left: Behind
the high altar
a way is
designed to
allow
processions
or pilgrims
to move
round the
cathedral:
Troyes, France.
below:
Through the
Church, the
way to
salvation:
this belief
seems to be
expressed in
the Paradise
Portal,
Paderborn,
Germany.

left: The
relics which
drew
pilgrims
were often
concealed in
tombs or
jewelled
cases, but all
could — and
still can —
see the
Black Virgin
of Montserrat,
Spain.

The Pope

The bishops were the officers who held the Church together, but there were others above them. Over each group of bishops there was an archbishop, and in every kingdom there would be one archbishop who was senior to the rest. In England there were two archbishops. The map on page 11 shows which bishoprics were within the province of each archbishop. Canterbury was senior to York.

People who were not satisfied by a judgment in a bishop's court could appeal to the archbishop. People who were still dissatisfied could go still further, to Rome, to the court of the Pope himself. Nobody could go further than that – at least, not in this world.

The Pope or, as he was sometimes called, the Vicar of St Peter (or of Christ), was head of the entire Western Church. He ruled it on behalf of God. No man could be above him.

Think of what this means. Everyone believed that when Christ had finally ascended to Heaven He had left St Peter to act as His representative, or vicar. He gave him even the keys of Heaven and Hell. St Peter was the first Pope, and every Pope afterwards inherited his powers. Remember how important this had seemed to King Oswy at the Synod of Whitby. The Pope spoke with the voice of God. From him, through the archbishops and bishops and priests, God's commands came to ordinary laymen.

Any man who was not a churchman was a layman. Even a great layman, count or earl, duke or king, was supposed to treat the Church with respect and obedience. Enemies of the Church, it was thought, were enemies of God.

This was something that even the toughest warriors and the proudest kings feared. If they were to die while still enemies of God, they would surely go straight to Hell. And this was certain if they had been cut off from the Church as a punishment, or excommunicated. Once a man had been excommunicated the Church would have nothing to do with him. He could attend no service. He could not be married. If he were to die, there would be no last sacraments or decent burial for him. What was more, he would be spurned by his friends, for anyone trying to help him would incur the same dreadful punishment. On earth and in Heaven there was no hope for anyone who was under the curse of the Church.

With a power like this in his hand, a Pope would sometimes

St Peter with his keys, shown by an Italian sculptor at the end of the Middle Ages.

An excommunicant (*below*) was condemned to be an outcast in both this world and the next.

try to make himself the complete master of western Europe. Some Popes even thought that they had the right to remove a king if he behaved badly, and give the kingdom to someone else. Though in fact no Pope ever succeeded in doing quite that, many Popes were well able to put the fear of God, quite literally, into kings and nobles.

Archbishop Thomas Becket, shown in a stained glass window in Canterbury cathedral made a few years after his murder in 1170. His pallium is clearly visible, the narrow white cloth with crosses hanging from his neck.

From all over Europe people flocked to the papal court. Pilgrims came to visit the churches and relics of the Holy City; lawyers and their clients to plead their cases; archbishops to receive the pallium, the strip of cloth which was their badge of office; messengers with offerings of money from churches all over Christendom; great men seeking the Pope's aid, or perhaps permission to break one of the rules of the Church in some such matter as marrying a near relative. The Pope and his courtiers were tremendously busy. There had to be hundreds of officials to deal with all this work, to write letters and seal documents and record judgments and count money and make sure that all the laws and rules and regulations were kept up to date. In short, the Pope was the only ruler in Europe who had a real civil service, something like a modern government – or like the ancient government of imperial Rome a thousand years before.

Rome was no longer the Imperial City, and her ruler no longer enforced his authority with the sword. But Rome was still the heart of western Europe.

Monks

So far, we have been thinking about all those churchmen whose main job was to keep the Church going and to look after the laymen. There were thousands of other churchmen, and women, who wished to serve God without having anything to do with the ordinary everyday world of the laymen, where people were too often wicked, dishonest, greedy and violent. Such men and women became monks and nuns.

You will already have heard about St Benedict, and know that there was nothing new in this idea. In the Middle Ages, it became more important than ever. New orders were founded. Monasteries became bigger, new ones were built. In England alone there were more than 2,000 in the fourteenth century, and it was the same story all over Christendom. Most monks were Benedictine, following the Rule of St Benedict, or lived according to some very similar rule. By looking at a typical monastery we can learn much about the sort of life they led.

This picture of a monastery may at first seem a baffling

One king had a grander title than any of the others. He was the Holy Roman Emperor. You know how the Frankish king, Charles the Great, had become the first Holy Roman Emperor in AD 800 and how, long after his death, his empire had split. During the Middle Ages the Holy Roman Empire consisted of Germany and some of the near-by lands, and the emperor was elected by the most important German nobles. Sometimes there were fierce quarrels between Pope and emperor, for some emperors argued that the chief king in Christendom was just as important a servant of God as the Pope, though God had given him different duties to perform; against this the Pope would argue that unless he crowned him, the emperor did not have God's blessing. On the whole, it was the Pope who won these quarrels.

Durham was a cathedral served by monks, and most of the monastery buildings remain. The plan was a normal Benedictine one, slightly modified to suit the ground; for instance, the dormitory has been built on the western side of the cloister, and the great courtyard lies to the south.

Cluny was a great French monastery which became the centre of a revival of enthusiasm for the monastic life which spread all over Europe. The plan, based on excavations, shows it about 1050. It is typical of the way the parts of a big monastery were grouped.

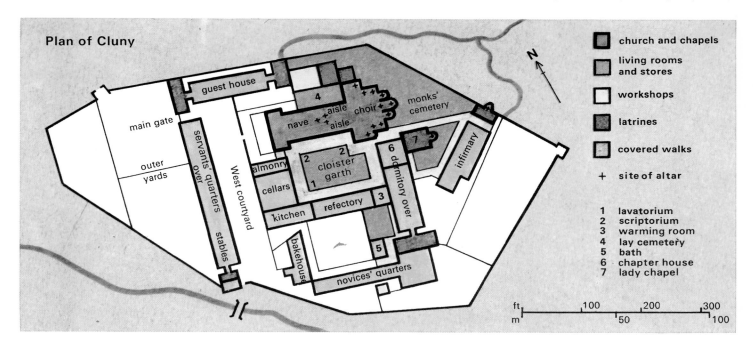

Plan of Cluny

- main gate
- outer yards
- guest house
- servants' quarters over
- West courtyard
- stables
- almonry
- cellars
- kitchen
- bakehouse
- cloister garth
- refectory
- novices' quarters
- nave
- aisle
- choir
- aisle
- monks' cemetery
- dormitory over
- infirmary

Legend:
- church and chapels
- living rooms and stores
- workshops
- latrines
- covered walks
- + site of altar

1. lavatorium
2. scriptorium
3. warming room
4. lay cemetery
5. bath
6. chapter house
7. lady chapel

ft | 100 | 200 | 300
m | 50 | 100

maze of buildings. But if we study a monastery methodically, one part at a time, we shall find that each part is easy to understand, and that all the pieces fit together sensibly.

The most important place, obviously, is the place for worship; the church. Like any other church, it would be built east–west, with the high altar at the east end. Next to this would be the choir, where the monks would assemble for services, and further west the nave, where outsiders might sometimes be admitted. On each side would be the aisles, often with extra altars. In the transepts, the 'cross' part of the church, there would be more chapels. All these chapels and altars were needed because many of the monks were priests as well, and every priest was bound to say Mass at least once a day.

Even a monk could not be in church all the time. For one thing, he needed sleep. Because some services were held in the middle of the night, however, the dormitory where the monks slept had to be near the church. Usually it was built upstairs, and there was a flight of stairs leading directly from the dormitory into the transept.

Monks had to eat, too, so a dining hall or refectory was built near the dormitory. It had to be big enough to take all the monks, and there was a pulpit on one side so that during meals the monks could listen to a reading from a religious book. Meals were simple and sparse, except on the great feast days.

A dining hall needs a kitchen near it, and a kitchen needs storage cellars. You can find them on the plan of the monastery. Water is needed, both for cooking and for washing. Often you can see near a refectory traces of a lavatorium, or washing-place, for the monks to use before meals. The Latin for 'to wash' is 'lavare'.

As for the places which are usually called lavatories nowadays, monasteries were quite well supplied. They were often built out over a stream, so that the filth would be carried away.

Many other rooms were needed. Every day the monks used to meet to discuss monastery business. This meeting was known as a Chapter, for each meeting began with a reading of a chapter of the Rule of the Order, and a Chapter House was built for it. Sometimes this was an oblong room under the dormitory, sometimes a separate octagonal building with a pointed roof and a strong central pillar. Among the other

far left: Night stairs, Hexham priory.
left: Refectory pulpit, Chester cathedral.
above: Lavatorium, Gloucester cathedral.

rooms there would be places for reading and writing – a scriptorium – and a library. There would also be one room with a fire, where the monks would be allowed to warm themselves for a short time each day. Most of the time they had to do without any heating.

As you can see from the plan, all these could be arranged in a square, with a covered walk running round the inside, and a lawn in the middle. The walk was called the cloister, and the lawn the cloister garth. Thus the church and cloister buildings – usually on the south side of the church, for protection against the coldest winds – formed the main part of the monastery, where the monks lived, prayed and worked.

The buildings beyond this group are easily explained. In the infirmary, sick monks could be given more comfort than was possible in their normal living quarters. The head of the monastery, who was called either the abbot or the prior, needed a separate house because he would often have business with outsiders, and the monks did not want strangers wandering about the cloisters. There were often barns, sheds, a forge, a mill, a house for servants, all outside the cloisters but within the monastery wall. There were guest houses, too, for monks sheltered travellers; rich travellers were expected to pay, but poor men were given alms, fed and sheltered free.

You may be noticing that, though they were shutting themselves away, the monks still had an influence on the people outside. In the early Middle Ages, monasteries were the only places where anyone studied or wrote books. They helped travellers and the poor. Monasteries themselves became rich, often holding villages and towns, because kings and lords so often tried to please God by giving lands to monasteries. Some monks were important farmers and landlords; in England the Cistercian monks became famous for their sheep-farming and wool. Often, too, a monastery would have the famous shrine of a saint, like St Albans, and pilgrims would come from far and near; many of the pilgrims would leave gifts. In England, though not in other countries, monasteries were frequently attached to cathedrals, because monks had such a good reputation that some bishops thought that they would perform the services better than other priests.

With all this interference from outside, it was often hard for the monks to live such strict lives as they had intended. So, from time to time, some monk would decide that his monastery was becoming rather soft and comfortable, and that he

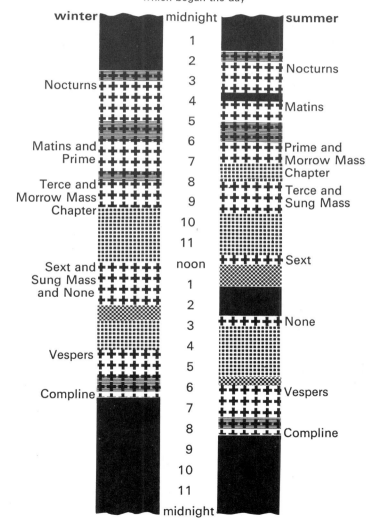

The Monk's timetable

prayer — reading and meditation / services in the church

work — including Chapter

physical needs — sleeping / eating

In both seasons Prime was the Canonical Hour (service) which began the day

winter — midnight — summer

Nocturns

Matins and Prime

Terce and Morrow Mass Chapter

Sext and Sung Mass and None

Vespers

Compline

(summer column) Nocturns / Matins / Prime and Morrow Mass Chapter / Terce and Sung Mass / Sext / None / Vespers / Compline

midnight

With small variations, the monastic timetable was the same all over Western Christendom. This example is from the 'Regularis Concordia', normal in England from the mid-tenth century onwards.

should begin a new order of monks, in which the rule would be harder, stricter. One of the most famous of these new orders began in 1098. They were called Cistercians, or White Monks, because they began at Cîteaux, in France, and wore garments of plain, undyed wool. They went to live in wild, wooded valleys where they would not be disturbed. You can see the sort of place from the picture. You may also notice that there are one or two new features in the plan of the monastery. This was largely because they allowed lay-brothers to join them. These were men who either would not or could not be sufficiently educated to become full monks and take part in the services, but who wanted to live a religious life and would do much of the work in and around the monastery. So the lay-brothers had their own refectory and dormitory on one side of the cloisters, while the monks had the rest.

The reason for the tower in such an odd place is quite different. At first the Cistercians would not have anything elaborate or ornamental about their monasteries; so there were no fine towers. But time went on, the monasteries became rich, and the old simplicity began to fade away. In this particular monastery the church had not been designed to

Fountains Abbey, Yorkshire, from the north west. The long building on the west side of the cloister is the lay brothers' refectory and dormitory. Because it takes up so much space, the monks' refectory is built out at right angles from the south side of the cloister; this was usual in Cistercian monasteries. On the photograph you can trace the course of the stream which supplied fresh water at one end and swept away sewage at the other.

take a big central tower, so, as the usual place was not strong enough, the tower was built at the end of the north transept.

This sort of thing did tend to happen. An order would begin very strictly, but would slowly relax.

One order never relaxed. These monks were the Carthusians, who had been founded in 1084. The picture shows how different their monasteries were from the others. This was because they lived like hermits, each monk in his own little house, with his workroom, bedroom, tiny chapel and garden. Except when they met for services in the chapel, the monks saw nobody else, and there were far fewer services in this order than in the others; you can see that the chapel is small and simple, compared with the other monastery churches.

Mount Grace Priory, Yorkshire, from the west; a drawing to show what it probably looked like at the end of the Middle Ages. North of the church lies the main cloister, surrounded by the monks' cells. South are a few more cells, then the courtyard with barns, stables and, by the gate, the guest house.

left: Cut-away drawing of what a cell may have been like. Upstairs is the workroom, downstairs the living room with two tiny rooms, bedroom and chapel, opening from it. One covered way leads to a latrine at the bottom of the garden, the other contains the fresh-water tap.

21

Mount Grace as it is today.

These monks did not even see the servant who brought their meals. As the photograph shows, there was a serving hatch built so that the monk could see no more than a hand putting in a plate. It may have been because they shut themselves away so very completely that the Carthusians were able to remain strict. The Carthusians were so strict that they were always deeply respected, and always remained a rather small order.

A serving hatch in what remains of the Charterhouse — a common name for a Carthusian monastery — in London. The photograph represents the extent of a monk's everyday contact with the outside world.

Friars

Dominic and the Pope's envoys.

If you had asked a monk what use he was to other people, his answer would have been simple. He was praying for them, so that God would have mercy on them. This, as most people would have agreed in the Middle Ages, was one of the best things that one man could do for another. As for ordinary day-to-day work in the parishes, this was the job of the parish priests.

Some churchmen, however, began to think that something more was needed.

Such a man was Dominic, a Spaniard born about 1170. When he was a young priest he had to go on a journey through the south of France, where many of the people had taken up a new sort of Christianity. In the opinion of the Church, anyone who broke away and thought differently from the Pope and bishops was an enemy of God. People like this were known as heretics, from a Greek word meaning 'people who choose'. The Church tried to make them change their minds, by persuasion or, if that failed, by force. These particular heretics lived near the city of Albi, and were called 'Albigensians'. On this journey Dominic met some priests whom the Pope had sent to persuade the Albigensians. They were riding along, splendidly dressed, attended by servants, expecting everybody to bow down before them. And the Albigensians had taken no notice. Dominic was not surprised, but he was angry. He spoke thus: 'How can you expect to succeed, with all this wealth and pride? You ought to practise what you preach. You will never win over the heretics unless you behave simply. The heretic preachers know that better than you do! Throw away your riches, be like the disciples of Jesus, go without money or food or shoes, and preach the truth.'

Dominic himself did exactly that. He began to wander from village to village, town to town, begging his bread and owning nothing but his white gown and black cloak. Wherever he went, he preached. He was himself a very well-educated man, and he could argue with the cleverest. Yet he also knew how important it was to be able to explain things simply to ordinary peasants and workmen, and to show them that churchmen were not really fond of wealth, comfort and splendour.

Other priests soon joined Dominic, to live and work as he did. Dominic was offered bishoprics, but he refused to become a bishop. His task was to go about preaching, not to rule from a cathedral. The Pope heard about him and at last, in 1216, allowed him to found a new order.

Dominic's order was called the Order of Preachers, and his men were not monks. They had houses, but these were not monasteries; instead, they were bases from which the preachers could go out on their journeys, and centres where they could study and learn to do their job better. The Dominicans, as they were called, devoted their lives to two things, studying and preaching. They called themselves simply Friars, which means Brothers.

This picture in the church of St Francis, Pescia, was painted only a few years after the saint's death. Around his portrait are some of his miracles.
left: 1 God marks Francis with the stigmata (the scars of Christ's wounds).
2 Francis preaches to the birds.
3 At Francis' tomb a noblewoman is cured of a fistula of the breast.
right: 1 Francis cures cripples, who include a leper carrying a wooden clapper to warn people not to come near him.
2 Francis cures a man of gout by bathing his foot.
3 At Francis' tomb evil spirits fly out of the man they have been possessing.

24

During the very years when St Dominic was striving against the heretics and founding his preaching friars, in Italy another man was beginning another order of friars. St Francis began as a rich, gay young man of the town of Assisi, merry and generous, without a care in the world. He was always to remain happy and kind, but he became the poorest of the poor. During an illness he began to think seriously about what he ought to do with his life, and at last decided that he should give up all his wealth. He became a beggar, giving all the money he begged to rebuild churches. Then he suddenly thought of some of the words of the Gospel: 'Go rather to the lost sheep of the house of Israel, and as you go, preach, saying "The Kingdom of Heaven is at hand"' . . . Get you no gold, nor silver, nor brass in your purses; no wallet for your journey, neither two coats, nor shoes, nor staff.'

Francis did so.

With those who soon began to follow him, he wandered about Italy, begging and working for food, sleeping where shelter was offered or in little huts of branches and mud, asking everyone to think more about God. Above all, Francis and his friends taught kindness among men, and even among all living things. They nursed the sick, even lepers, and there are stories about how birds and wild animals sensed that Francis would do them no harm, and came and listened while he preached.

The sheer goodness and happiness of these poor men made them very popular. Within ten years of his starting out, Francis had 5,000 people trying to imitate his way of life. When they became an order, rules had to be made and houses built, but still the spirit of St Francis inspired his followers. They called themselves the Friars Minor, or Lesser Brothers, and wore a plain grey garment.

The Blackfriars of St Dominic and the Greyfriars of St Francis spread all over Christendom, and even beyond, within a few years. They preached on village greens and on the steps of market crosses. They taught in colleges and universities. They were sent on missions to the lands of the non-Christians in Asia and to Egypt.

Nothing quite like this had been seen inside Western Christendom before. They had a great deal of success, and were greatly respected. Yet, as the years went on, what had happened to the orders of monks happened to the orders of friars. They lost their fire. They began to wear shoes and good clothes, and their friaries became comfortable places to live in. Being a friar, like being a monk, was too often just a respectable way of making a safe living and keeping on the right side of God at the same time. Most of the friars at the end of the Middle Ages were probably decent enough men who did a certain amount of good, but they were not very much like Dominic and Francis.

The dream of Innocent III, painted by Giotto. The Pope dreams that the tottering Church is saved by St Francis. This is one of a series of paintings in the mighty church built to honour 'the little poor man', who rejected all possessions and wealth, in his home town of Assisi.

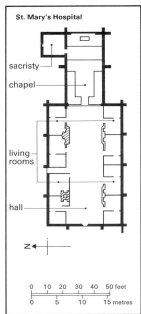

St. Mary's Hospital

sacristy

chapel

living rooms

hall

Z

0 10 20 30 40 50 feet
0 5 10 15 metres

Inside St Mary's Hospital, Chichester, looking towards the chapel from the space between the two rows of dwellings. This building was erected about 1290.

below left: St Cross, Winchester, was founded in 1136 for thirteen poor old men. It has a fine Norman church and many later buildings, including the half-timbered infirmary shown here.

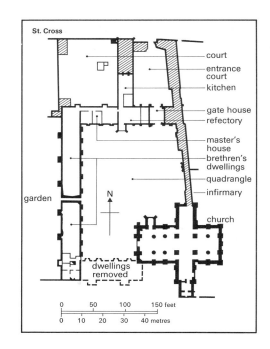

St. Cross

court
entrance court
kitchen
gate house
refectory
master's house
brethren's dwellings
quadrangle
infirmary
church

garden

N

dwellings removed

0 50 100 150 feet
0 10 20 30 40 metres

Charity

The friars were most famous for working among the poor and the sick, but they were not the only ones. The Church had always taught that it was good to help the needy, and there were always many people in misery – victims of bad harvests, war or robbery; widows, orphans, old people; sufferers from illness or injury. There were always people starving, ill-clad and cold, homeless, in pain.

Kings, lords and rich men often gave food and clothes to the poor. Churchmen usually helped. Some rich men, however, decided to set up special houses where sick or aged people could be cared for. These were called hospitals.

Nowadays we think of hospitals as places connected with medical care and cure, but in the Middle Ages the hospital was much more a shelter for those who could not look after themselves. Even today there are many illnesses which doctors cannot cure, and then there were far more. All too often the only thing that anyone could do for the ill was to try to make them fairly comfortable.

One of the most famous hospitals in London, St Bartholomew's, was founded in 1123 by a rich churchman who had just recovered from a serious illness. Most cities had such hospitals, and sometimes there was a special leper hospital outside the town walls for those wretched untouchables. Most of the hospitals, either for the sick or the old, which were founded in the Middle Ages, have been destroyed or damaged or very much altered, but opposite you can see good examples. The one at the top is for old women. Each side of the hall is divided into small apartments, one for every old woman, and there is a chapel at the far end. This hospital was founded in 1172, or perhaps earlier.

In Norwich the Hospital of St Giles was founded in 1246, and it served to shelter three different sorts of needy people: 'thirty poor and decrepit chaplains', thirty poor people, and seven poor scholars. This reminds us that schools, too, were founded for the benefit of the poor, but we shall think about these later.

Christians were expected to perform the Seven Corporal Acts of Mercy. The last of these, burying the dead, is here depicted in a fifteenth-century Flemish book entitled: *Blessed shall be the merciful.*

eeding the hungry.

Giving drink to the thirsty.

Clothing the naked.

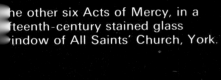

he other six Acts of Mercy, in a
fteenth-century stained glass
indow of All Saints' Church, York.

In towns clubs of merchants and craftsmen, called guilds, usually set up charities for their own members, and the miseries and dangers of poverty were rather less for people who belonged to guilds. Apart from these, there would be in most towns a number of places to assist the unfortunate; hospitals, friaries, special chapels in the bigger churches. It was thanks to the Church that such things were done, for the Church urged Christians to perform the Seven Corporal Acts of Mercy. You can see what these were from this stained-glass window, made in York in the fifteenth century.

Learning

In order to do its work the Church needed educated men, and therefore had to have schools and colleges. Great kings like Charles of the Franks and Alfred of the English had sometimes encouraged their noblemen to become educated, but mainly it was the Church which, for hundreds of years, kept education alive. A peasant or a warrior could do his job without knowing how to read or write. As for kings and great lords, they found it easier to employ churchmen to do their reading and writing for them.

There was so much of this work to be done that some churchmen spent all their working lives in the employment of a king or lord. In the Middle Ages, the word 'clerk' meant simply 'churchman', and the modern meaning has come because only churchmen were able to do what we would now call 'white-collar' (or 'clerical') jobs.

In many big churches, cathedrals and monasteries there were schools for boys who wanted to become churchmen. Many boys did want to; some wished only to serve God, but others may have been more interested in the fact that it was only by becoming a churchman that the son of a peasant or workman could become great and powerful. At these schools the boys would learn to speak, read and write in Latin. All educated men used Latin for any serious business, no matter what their native language was. The boys would also be taught how to study and discuss religious books.

Gradually it became fairly common for great and rich men to found schools. Some of those founded in England in the fourteenth and fifteenth centuries have become famous, like that which Bishop William of Wykeham began at Winchester and that which King Henry VI began at Eton. Such schools

were intended as works of charity, to give a good education to poor boys.

Those who wished to go on studying after they had learned all they could at school used sometimes to seek particularly good teachers who worked in other towns and countries. Some towns became famous, and both teachers and pupils gathered there. These great schools were called universities. Because all used Latin, there was little difficulty if scholars wished to move, say, from the University of Paris to that of Salamanca, or Oxford, or Mainz, or Salerno, or Prague, or Cracow.

A lesson in progress, late fifteenth century. This illustration is from one of the new printed books which were invented as the Middle Ages were ending, and which were to make education easier in future.

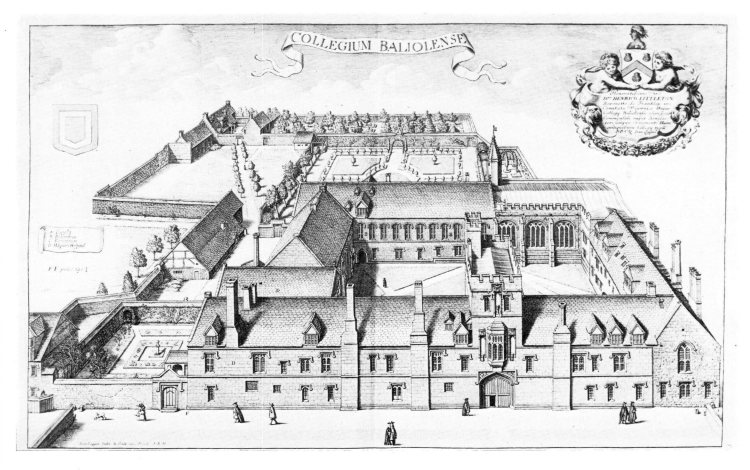

COLLEGIUM BALIOLENSE

Balliol College, Oxford, founded in 1263. The late medieval plan is seen intact in this seventeenth-century view.

Some places became specially famous for certain subjects, like Bologna for law and Montpellier for medicine. In some universities groups of teachers and students would club together to find a place to live, instead of trying to use lodgings or inns. These places were called colleges, and many of them exist today. With its chapel and dining hall and square court or quadrangle – occasionally with cloisters – an old college could remind you a little of a monastery.

The Church helped in founding colleges, too. Some were founded by bishops, others by kings, queens and lords, so that poor scholars should have somewhere to live. The story about the college in the picture above is that a powerful lord, John Balliol, had a quarrel with the bishop of Durham, and lost. The bishop punished him by beating him publicly and ordering him to perform a work of charity. The college was the result.

In time, people came to realise that a good education was well worth having, even if they were not going to be clerks. Knowledge might be useful, and to be taught how to think clearly was certainly very useful. Even noblemen began to go to universities. The Church went on controlling what was taught, but by the fifteenth century schools and colleges had grown so strong that they hardly needed the Church to support and protect them any longer.

2. The feudal lords

The ruling class

If the great number of medieval churches tells us of one side of life in those centuries, the castles tell us of another.

The Church may have preached kindness and peace, but everybody who could afford it lived behind a strong wall. The men who ruled Europe thought that it was better to fight than to work.

In the Middle Ages there were three classes, or 'estates', of people. There were the churchmen. Then there were the nobles – kings, lords, knights – who ruled and fought. Finally there were the great majority who worked for their living. You already know about the churchmen. Now it is time for us to look at the ruling class.

The lord of the manor

You saw on page 10 how, as far as his religious life was concerned, every peasant belonged to a parish, and had to attend the parish church and help to pay for it and for the priest. For ordinary, everyday things, for his life and work in this world, the peasant belonged to a manor, and had to obey the lord of the manor.

Sometimes there might be two small villages in one parish; sometimes there might be two parishes in one village. In just the same way, there could be one, or two, or even three manors in one village, and vice versa. Often, though, it was simply one manor covering one village, and it is simplest to explain how manors worked with this sort of example.

The lord of the manor was supposed to hold all the land in the manor, and the peasants had to pay him for whatever land they worked on. They did not pay in money, but by working for the lord during part of each week, and by giving him some of their crops and animals. Many of these villagers were serfs: that is, they were not allowed to leave the manor without the lord's permission, and he could bring them back and punish them if they ran away. On the other hand, as long as the villagers paid their dues, the lord could not throw them off their pieces of land. Also, it was the lord's duty to protect his people, in war and in peace.

The lord would usually live in a large house or a castle, and here he would hold the manor court. If there were any disputes between villagers – for instance, about how many animals a man could put out to graze on the common field – he would settle them according to what seemed the usual custom of the manor. If a villager had done anything wrong, the lord could punish him; usually this would be by a fine, because the right

Stokesay Castle, Shropshire, is a fortified manor house of about 1300. The half-timbered parts are later additions, the wall was probably higher and battlemented, and the moat is dry now; but the main block of buildings shows perfectly how all big houses were planned. The hall is the centre – as it had been in the days of the barbarian chieftains – with the lord's private rooms and stronghold at one end and the less important parts of the household at the other.

Plan of Stokesay Castle

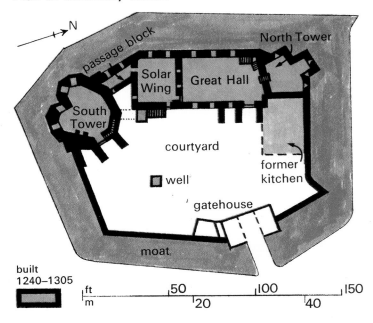

to hang wrongdoers was mostly reserved for the courts of the king or the most important lords.

The size of the lord's house or castle would depend on how rich he was. A rich lord who held several manors might have a real castle in one, and leave bailiffs in smaller houses to run his other manors. Also, many manors belonged to kings or earls, bishops or monasteries, and these would employ bailiffs to look after the manors. Even the smallest lord, however, in the poorest manor, would feel happier if he had a house strong enough to be defended.

What was the lord of the manor afraid of?

To begin with, there were his own villagers. Many a lord made himself unpopular by his pride and greed. Besides, in a newly conquered country, like England after 1066, there were bitter feelings against the new masters, with their strange ways and foreign speech. All over England the Normans threw up castles of earth and wood, which were quick to build and quite strong. When life was more settled, and the lords had time and wealth to spare, they often replaced their motte-and-bailey castles by stone buildings.

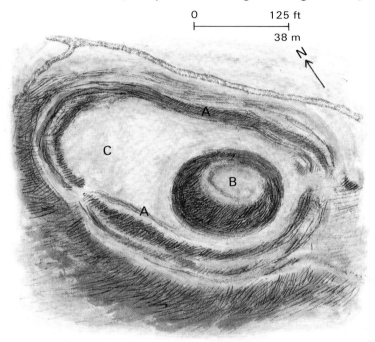

The Motte of Urr, Kirkcudbrightshire. The photograph, taken from the east, shows the earthworks today, and the bird's-eye drawing explains the arrangement of ditches and ramparts. When castles of this type were in use, the earth ramparts (A) were crowned by strong wooden walls. On top of the motte (B) stood a wooden tower with a palisade at its foot. Within the bailey (C) there would have been sheds, stables, workshops and living quarters—sometimes even a whole village.

Even if the peasants were friendly and loyal, there was danger. Other lords, especially strong ones, might be greedy. It was easy for a powerful lord to invent some claim to the lands of a weaker neighbour; and, unless he feared the king or the king's sheriff (the officer who represented the king in the shire or county) he might try to grab what he claimed by force.

Finally, there was the danger of real war. Rival princes might fight for the crown, and begin a civil war. When this happened in England in the 1130s and 1140s, between Stephen and Matilda, it was not safe to be without a stronghold, and many castles were built then. The next king, Henry II, was strong, and realised that castles might easily be held against the king's men if there were a rebellion, so he had many of them pulled down. A lord had to ask the king's permission before he could crenellate, or put battlements on his house.

There was also danger from other kingdoms. An army or raiding party could cross the border long before the king or any of his great nobles could bring men to stop it. Looting and burning were common. So anyone within striking distance of an unfriendly kingdom would try to have a strong house. On the Anglo-Scottish border, during the fourteenth and fifteenth centuries, pele towers like this were built; as you see, even churchmen felt that they needed such defence against the lawless men who infested the borderlands.

We have taken examples from England, but the same conditions could be found in many parts of western Europe. In many kingdoms there was much more fighting than in England.

From all this, you may be beginning to think that lords were constantly being attacked by one enemy or another. That would not be true. For much of the time everything would be quiet, and many of the most famous castles never saw any serious fighting at all. Nevertheless, just as people today think it safest to be insured, a lord had to be ready for trouble. He was also supposed to protect his peasants. He had his duties and his worries.

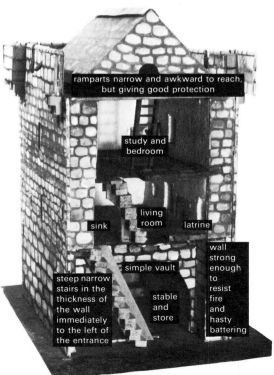

ramparts narrow and awkward to reach, but giving good protection

study and bedroom

sink

living room

latrine

wall strong enough to resist fire and hasty battering

simple vault

steep narrow stairs in the thickness of the wall immediately to the left of the entrance

stable and store

The fourteenth-century Vicar's Pele Tower, standing at the edge of the churchyard, by the market place, at Corbridge, Northumberland. The model is opened to show how the rooms were arranged.

34

Barons and knights

The lord of the manor held the village, but he did not own it, any more than the peasants owned the land which they held from him. The lord held it because he served another lord who had handed it over to him. When he received his land from this other lord, the lord of the manor came as you see in the picture, and swore to serve the lord who was giving him the land by fighting for him. This ceremony was called doing homage and swearing fealty. In return, the greater lord promised to protect the lord of the manor. The greater one was called the 'lord' of the smaller one, and the smaller one was called the 'vassal' of the greater one. Land held on these conditions was known as a 'fief'.

In the same way, the greater lord himself might be the vassal of a still more powerful lord, and so it could go on until somebody was the vassal of the king. So everyone was the vassal of somebody else; even some kings were vassals of others, as you will see.

Vassals paid for their fiefs, not only by fighting in person for their lords but by bringing properly equipped horsemen,

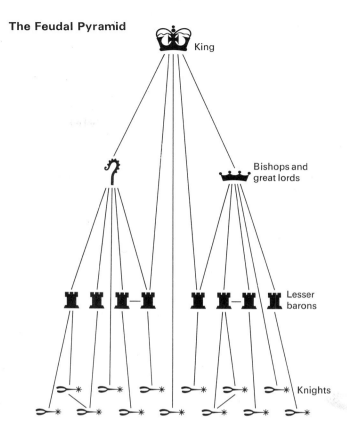

The Feudal Pyramid

King

Bishops and great lords

Lesser barons

Knights

It was possible for quite small tenants to hold lands directly of a great lord, even of a king himself; or for a man to hold lands of two or more others, including men of no higher rank than himself.

'Inmixtio manum', the ceremony when a vassal placed his hands between his lord's, and they swore to keep faith. From a fifteenth-century German chronicle.

or knights, with them. Bishops and abbots who held land, usually from the king, were not forced to fight themselves, because they were churchmen and must not shed blood; but they had to pay the fair number of knights just like anybody else, because no king could afford to do without all the soldiers which the lands could support. The number of knights which each lord owed would depend on how much land he held and what he had agreed with his own lord. A very small lord might be expected to bring only one knight – himself. You can get from the diagram a very simplified idea of how it all worked.

There was a time limit on the service vassals owed each year. In England this was forty days. If the king wanted to keep his vassals in the army for longer than this he was entitled to do so, but he had to pay them.

This system of holding land by military service is called Feudalism. What it meant in practice was that the king could call up his vassals, who would bring their vassals, who would bring their vassals, and so on, until there was a knight for every manor in the country. But usually the king would not want all of his knights in the army at the same time. When they were not with the army, these knights ruled their manors and kept order in the country.

It may seem to you that only one knight from each manor is not much. That is true, but you must bear in mind two things. First, we are not talking about foot-soldiers, and there would be many more of them. Second, knights were very special and expensive soldiers. They wore full armour, and were mounted. As you can see from this series of pictures, the armour became more elaborate as the Middle Ages went on. Mail was gradually replaced by cunningly forged plates of steel. It became ever more expensive. Then the horses had to be specially strong and fierce. There had to be servants to look after the knight, his armour and weapons and horse, and they, too, needed horses. There had to be tents sometimes, and food. So you can see that a man had to be well off before he could afford to be a knight. Only a very great lord, or the king himself, would be rich enough to keep knights in his household as a guard.

William Marshal,
Earl of Pembroke, 1146–1219.

These drawings are based on the figures on the tombs of great lords, and can be taken to show high-quality armour at the time of each man's death.

Hugh le Despenser,
Earl of Winchester, 1261–1326.

Robert de Vere,
Earl of Oxford and Duke of Dublin,
Knight of the Garter,
1362–92.

William de la Pole,
Earl and later Duke of Suffolk,
Knight of the Garter,
1396–1450.

Though there were far more soldiers of other sorts in medieval armies, the knights were always thought to be far more important than the other troops. The outcome of a battle depended on these heavy steel warriors and their fearful charge. The men who ruled the battlefields in war and the villages in peace were, with the churchmen, the most important set of people in medieval Europe. They had different titles, according to their importance; working downwards from the king himself, there were dukes, marquises, earls and counts, barons and plain knights. All those above the rank of plain knight are sometimes grouped together as 'lords' or 'barons', but, great or small, they all belonged to the feudal ruling class, and felt quite different from ordinary people.

In war, the important thing was the lord a man followed, not the nation to which he belonged. A French knight or baron thought of himself as being the same sort of man as a German or English or Spanish or Italian knight or baron. In battle, these men would capture one another, and the prisoners would be held to ransom, being treated all the time as honoured guests. Sometimes a captive knight would even be released in order to raise his ransom money, or if he were ill or wounded, after promising to return to captivity if he failed to find the money or when he had recovered; gentlemen could be trusted to keep their word. (Meanwhile, common soldiers were simply slaughtered.) Knights and barons married one another's daughters, after careful discussions about how much dowry the bride would bring her husband. They never intermarried with peasants and townsmen; unless, perhaps, the townsman was very rich indeed. Even if one of them had to be executed, he would be beheaded with a sword or axe, though rope was good enough for ordinary criminals.

Barons and knights normally had two main interests; warfare and land. If they were good at war, they would get more land, either by conquering it or as a reward from their king. The more land they had, the more vassals they had and the stronger they were for war. The two things went together. We saw on page 32 how everyone who could manage it had his own castle. Many were small, but a really great lord might build a spectacular fortress-palace like Warwick castle. In lands where there was not a strong king, enormous numbers of castles can still be seen. In the part of the Rhineland shown here, there is a castle on almost every hill-top.

The lordly halls and towers of Warwick Castle. A nineteenth-century engraving, picturesque but accurate.

Pfalz Castle, in the midst of the Rhine, with a castle-crowned hill beyond it. Another nineteenth-century engraving.

The Clare Family

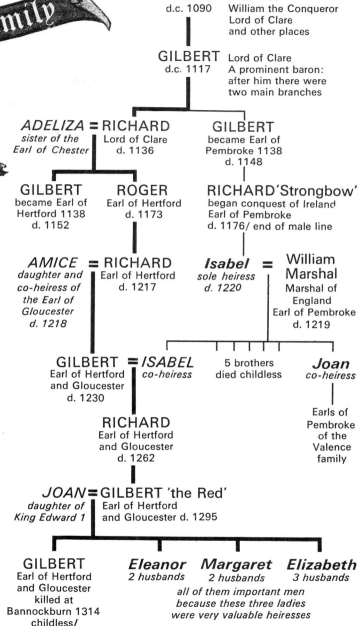

RICHARD
d.c. 1090
came with William the Conqueror
Lord of Clare and other places

GILBERT
d.c. 1117
Lord of Clare
A prominent baron:
after him there were two main branches

ADELIZA = RICHARD
sister of the Earl of Chester — Lord of Clare d. 1136

GILBERT
became Earl of Pembroke 1138
d. 1148

GILBERT
became Earl of Hertford 1138
d. 1152

ROGER
Earl of Hertford
d. 1173

RICHARD 'Strongbow'
began conquest of Ireland
Earl of Pembroke
d. 1176/ end of male line

AMICE = RICHARD
daughter and co-heiress of the Earl of Gloucester d. 1218 — Earl of Hertford d. 1217

Isabel = William Marshal
sole heiress d. 1220 — Marshal of England Earl of Pembroke d. 1219

GILBERT = ISABEL
Earl of Hertford and Gloucester d. 1230 — *co-heiress*

5 brothers
died childless

Joan
co-heiress

Earls of Pembroke of the Valence family

RICHARD
Earl of Hertford and Gloucester
d. 1262

JOAN = GILBERT 'the Red'
daughter of King Edward 1 — Earl of Hertford and Gloucester d. 1295

GILBERT
Earl of Hertford and Gloucester
killed at Bannockburn 1314
childless/ end of male line

Eleanor
2 husbands

Margaret
2 husbands

Elizabeth
3 husbands

all of them important men because these three ladies were very valuable heiresses

The other main way of getting land was through marriage. If a vassal died before his children had grown up, his lord had to look after them and their land until they were old enough to do it themselves. If the dead man had left only daughters to inherit his lands, there was usually a rush to marry them. It was the duty of the lord who was their guardian to look after them properly, and to see that they were suitably married. But it was tempting to a guardian to make a profit, and sometimes he would marry off an heiress to the highest bidder. There was little romance about marriage among the knights and barons; it was a serious matter of business. A family which made a few fortunate marriages could become very powerful indeed.

If a family died out completely, its fiefs went back to the lord, and he could either give them to someone else or keep them in his own hands.

In all this there was one very big disadvantage, from the king's point of view. You may be able to work it out from the diagram on page 35. Who really controlled the knights? Some of the great lords had so many vassals that a few of them, if they could rely on the loyalty of their vassals, might be strong enough to quarrel with the king and win. In fact, this happened fairly often in most of the kingdoms of Europe and, as we shall see later, kings of England had trouble with their barons.

A simplified table omitting many brothers, sisters, wives. The senior branch (on this side) made some very good marriages. Eventually all the property of both branches went with heiresses.

THE KING AND HIS PEERS

THE KING AND HIS PEOPLE

The greatest of the lords

In most of the kingdoms of Europe there were some very great barons, and they were often warlike and greedy. Even if some of them would have preferred a quiet life, they had no choice. They must be warriors as long as there were others ready to rob them. Trouble-makers can always prevent their neighbours from living in peace.

It is the job of the government to make sure that trouble-makers are not allowed to do this. You will remember that there had been governments which knew how to do it, especially the Roman Empire with its 'Pax Romana' and Roman Law. In the Middle Ages it was very different. Kings had to struggle to keep their barons under control.

The knights and barons still had many of the ideas of the old barbarian warriors – loyalty to their lords, keeping their promises, fighting rather than working, looking down on people who earned a peaceful living. Another of the ideas of the barbarian warriors had been that the king was the leader of a band of free fighting men; the king was not the all-powerful master, as the Roman emperors had been. In the Middle Ages the barons kept an independent spirit. They thought of the king as one of themselves who had been lucky. After all, how had William the Conqueror become a king? Or Robert Bruce? They had been no more than barons at first. Besides, many barons were related to the king; it is not always easy to feel tremendous respect for one's nephew or brother-in-law.

In some countries the position of the king was especially weak. In Germany, when a Holy Roman Emperor died, the next one was elected by the chief barons. In the Spanish kingdom of Aragon the nobles swore loyalty to the king thus: 'We, who are as good as you, swear to you, who are no better than we, to accept you as our king and sovereign lord, provided that you accept all our liberties and laws; but if not, not.' Perhaps this was being rather more brutally frank than in most countries, but barons everywhere had a similar notion at the backs of their minds, like the English barons who drew up Magna Carta. They would put up with just so much interference from the king, but if he went beyond what the barons thought was right, then there might be fighting,

In England, lords are often referred to as 'peers'. 'Peer' means 'equal'. These people were supposed to be the equals,

ulhnac honox et opix fozratiomus.tit

The coronation of
Charles V of
France, from a
fourteenth-
century French
manuscript.

Used in the coronation of French kings, this porphyry
vase with eagle-shaped gold mounts was kept in the
royal abbey of St Denis from the early twelfth century.

not only of one another, but of the king.

Being a king in the Middle Ages was not easy, yet the king
had some things on his side.

First, remember what you read on page 35. All the barons
had sworn loyalty, and that meant something to those men.
A baron would not like to break his oath unless the king had
given him an excuse.

Next, the king had been crowned and anointed by the
Church, and in a way that made him sacred.

Then, though a king could not raise taxes as easily as an
ancient Roman emperor or a modern government, he was
richer than any of his barons. He had more lands, castles,
knights; sometimes very many more. As a result, he found it
easier to borrow money when he needed to hire more soldiers.
He was the most powerful man in the kingdom.

Most important of all, many people always preferred to
have a strong king rather than a pack of quarrelsome barons.
Most of the barons and knights themselves probably felt
like this, especially if they were afraid of greedy neighbours.
Common people in villages and towns almost certainly did.
As merchants in towns became richer, they were able to give
the king more help to keep the country safe for trade.

The kings did their best to rule their countries, and later in
this book you will be able to see how some of them succeeded
or failed. In England, for example, the royal judges and courts
gradually took over most of the serious cases from the feudal
courts of the barons. Some kings were good men, and some
were not, but their success or failure depended on whether or
not the barons would obey them. Goodness had less to do with
this than strength and determination.

In England the Norman kings used to hold three great
feasts each year when they wore their crowns: Christmas at
Gloucester, Easter at Winchester, Whitsuntide at Westminster.
There they met their chief barons. The king could watch the
barons, and the barons could take a good look at the king.
The peace of England depended on what they saw.

3. Religion and the warriors

The Holy Wars

Proud as they were, and convinced of their own superiority over common people, the feudal lords and knights feared God and therefore respected the Church. They often gave or left lands or money to churches or monasteries, and the Church tried to improve their behaviour in two ways especially.

First, obviously, no good Christian should spend his time quarrelling, fighting, looting and ill-treating people who were weaker than himself. A Christian warrior should defend and show kindness to the weak.

Second, a Christian should fight only in a good cause. He could fight in self-defence, or to protect people who were being wrongly attacked; above all, he should fight for the Church against heathens.

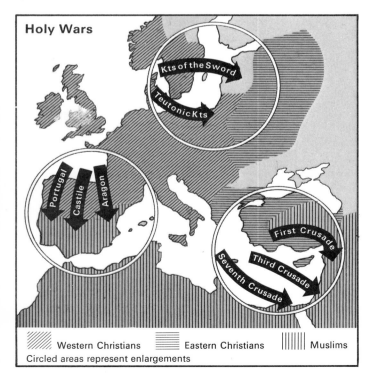

Holy Wars

Kts of the Sword
Teutonic Kts
Portugal
Castile
Aragon
First Crusade
Third Crusade
Seventh Crusade

///// Western Christians   ≡≡≡ Eastern Christians ||||| Muslims
Circled areas represent enlargements

Anyone who wished to go to war could easily find some heathen to fight. The Germans and Spaniards, as you see from the map, had plenty on their own borders. German knights pushed eastwards against those Slav and Baltic tribes which were still pagan. In Spain the sons of those Christians who had fled to the northern mountains when the Muslims swept over the land were gathering strength and pushing southwards. These two wars went on for centuries, until there were no more heathens on the shore of the Baltic, and no more Muslims in Spain. Knights and barons from other lands sometimes came to help the Spanish and German knights. These Holy Wars, however, were not so famous as the struggle to take and hold the Holy Land.

The First Crusade

In the seventh century the Arabs had carried their new faith of Islam, the religion of Allah and of the Prophet Muhammad, over the whole of the Middle East. Among the lands they conquered was Palestine. You probably remember that these Arabs were quite tolerant to the Jews and Christians, who both looked on Jerusalem as the holiest of all cities, and allowed them to come on pilgrimages.

THE COMING OF THE TURKS. Matters remained like that until the middle of the eleventh century, when there came upon the scene a new wave of nomad conquerors from the vast plains of central Asia. These were the Seljuk Turks, great fighters and looters, like other nomad horsemen you have heard of. There were two important, rich, civilised states in their way. One was the Muslim Caliphate of Baghdad, the other was the Christian Empire of Byzantium – the Eastern Roman Empire, as it still called itself. The Seljuk Turks became Muslims themselves, and took over many lands from the civilised Arabs, including the Holy Land. At the same time the Turks defeated the Byzantine army so completely at Manzikert that they were able to overrun most of Asia Minor.

THE APPEALS FOR HELP. These two victories led in turn to two appeals for help. The emperor in Byzantium appealed to the Pope. He led the Eastern Christian Church, while the Pope led the Western Church, but there was no serious quarrel between them and he knew that the Western Christians would not like to see Muslims conquer any more Christians. He knew

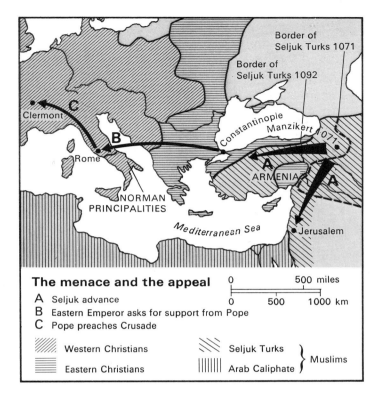

The menace and the appeal

A Seljuk advance
B Eastern Emperor asks for support from Pope
C Pope preaches Crusade

0 ____ 500 miles
0 ___ 500 ___ 1000 km

▨ Western Christians   ▨ Seljuk Turks   ⎫
▤ Eastern Christians   ▥ Arab Caliphate   ⎬ Muslims
                                               ⎭

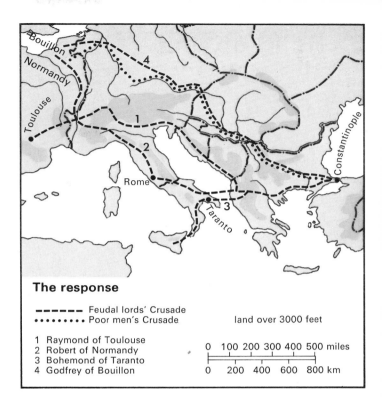

The response

– – – – – Feudal lords' Crusade
• • • • • • Poor men's Crusade   land over 3000 feet

1 Raymond of Toulouse
2 Robert of Normandy   0 100 200 300 400 500 miles
3 Bohemond of Taranto   0 200 400 600 800 km
4 Godfrey of Bouillon

that some Westerners were good warriors; he had Vikings in his bodyguard, and bands of wandering Normans had sometimes fought in his wars. So he hoped that the Pope would be able to persuade many warriors to come and enlist in his army, and help him to win back his lost provinces from the Turks. As it turned out, the emperor was going to get rather more than he had bargained for.

The other appeal was from Christian pilgrims who had been to Jerusalem. They had found the new rulers, the Turks, much worse than the Arabs. Turks had mocked, insulted, robbed and beaten them. Pilgrims who came back told shocking tales of how the Turks were behaving in the Holy Places. One pilgrim especially, called Peter the Hermit, aroused his hearers to fury, so that they began to think that it was time Christians took up arms to rescue the Holy Land from 'the infidels, the unbelievers'.

THE MEETING AT CLERMONT. Pope Urban II called a great meeting at Clermont, in France, and here on 26 November 1095, he made one of the most important speeches in history. This speech began the Crusades. He called for warriors to go to the Holy War, and, with cries of 'Deus lo volt!' (God wishes it!) thousands of men pinned upon their cloaks crosses which they made there and then from torn rags.

THE POOR MEN'S CRUSADE. The First Crusade, as it is known nowadays, was in two parts. The first to march were mobs of peasants and townsmen who, in the spring of 1096, were stirred by the furious words of Peter the Hermit. Badly armed and untrained, they straggled across Germany, where they massacred a few thousand Jews in revenge for the crucifixion of Jesus a thousand years before; then through Hungary and Bulgaria to Byzantium. Since they were God's warriors, they thought that they were entitled to be given free food and shelter, and often took what they wanted by force; so many of them were set upon and killed by enraged Hungarians and

Bulgarians. They behaved almost as badly when they reached Byzantium, and they were certainly not the experienced soldiers whom the emperor had hoped for. He ferried them across to Asia Minor, where they met the Turks. They were all wiped out before the end of autumn.

THE FEUDAL LORDS' CRUSADE. The barons and knights took longer. Though no kings came, there were some very great lords, including Hugh of Vermandois, the brother of the king of France, and Robert of Normandy, the eldest son of William the Conqueror. Such lords were able to attract thousands of knights and other soldiers. Making their way by different routes, as the map shows, the various forces assembled at Byzantium.

The Crusaders usually called Byzantium by its other name, Constantinople, and the Byzantines Greeks; it will be simpler if we use those names from now on.

This host of feudal warriors was a great problem to the Greek emperor. He had expected soldiers who would join his army and fight under his orders, but these lords from the West had other ideas. They intended to take the lands from the Turks and to keep them. They would please God by fighting Muslims, and reward themselves by remaining as rulers of the places they had liberated. So, from the start, there was misunderstanding between the Greek emperor and the Crusaders. Feelings were not made any more friendly because of the differences in church services and ceremonies between the Eastern Church and the Western Church. Because the leaders of the Crusade needed supplies and transport from the emperor, they promised to hand over to him the lands they took back from the Turks; but they promised very unwillingly.

Once they landed in Asia Minor, the Crusaders soon showed that they were excellent warriors. You can follow their advance on the map. They took Nicaea with the help of Greek engineers, and handed it over to the Greeks, as they had promised. At Dorylaeum they were lucky. The Crusading army was marching in two halves, several miles apart. One half was surrounded by the fast Turkish horsemen, who were shooting with their arrows the slow, heavy Crusaders, and were about to wipe them out. Then the other half of the Crusaders came up behind the Turks, who were now crushed between the two hosts of steel-clad knights.

This carving from a church in Limoges shows a knight who could well have gone on the First Crusade.

--- Main route
····· Godfrey of Bouillon

0   100   200 miles
0 100 200 300 km

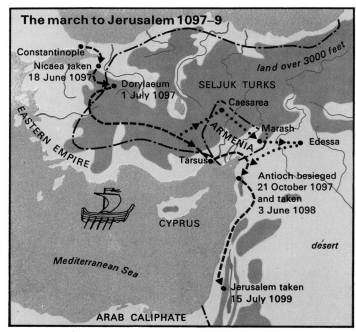

The march to Jerusalem 1097–9

Constantinople
Nicaea taken 18 June 1097
Dorylaeum 1 July 1097
land over 3000 feet
SELJUK TURKS
Caesarea
EASTERN EMPIRE
ARMENIA
Marash
Edessa
Tarsus
Antioch besieged 21 October 1097 and taken 3 June 1098
CYPRUS
desert
Mediterranean Sea
Jerusalem taken 15 July 1099
ARAB CALIPHATE

The Tower of David, Jerusalem. In 1099 some Muslims held out here after the city had fallen, until the crusaders gave them safe conduct. Later it became part of the King of Jerusalem's citadel.

The siege of the mighty city of Antioch looked hopeless, for the walls were too long to be surrounded and too strong to be stormed; and during the winter there was a desperate shortage of food in the Crusaders' camp, until ships from Genoa came to the rescue. At last, though, a Turkish officer turned traitor, and let the Crusaders into the tower he commanded. So the city fell. Even now the situation was grim, for the Crusaders were weak through casualties and desertions, while a very big Muslim army was marching to recapture Antioch. At this moment a miracle happened. A priest had a dream. As a result, he dug behind the high altar of the cathedral, and found the Holy Lance which had pierced the side of Christ on the Cross. It was very timely, so timely that some of the Crusaders had their doubts. Most of them, though, had no doubts. They took it as a sign that God was with them, and marched out and won an astonishing victory over the new Turkish army, scattering it completely.

At last they came to Jerusalem itself. The walls were strong, and the Muslims had seen to it that there was no food and water to be had outside the city; the wells were poisoned. The Crusaders tried to assault the walls, and were beaten back. Time was running out. A fresh Muslim army was on its way from Egypt, and the Crusade was doomed if the Christian army should be caught outside the walls of Jerusalem. The Crusaders built two high wooden towers on wheels, those siege-towers which look so awkward on pictures that it is hard to believe that they can ever have worked. From the drawbridge on top of one of these towers the Crusaders were able to force their way on to the walls of Jerusalem, and so they stormed the Holy City. Only men who had worked themselves into a state of fighting madness could have done it, and that is the only possible excuse for what happened next. The Christian soldiers charged through the streets and houses of Jerusalem, killing, killing, killing. They spared none, neither women nor children nor old people. After the massacre, covered with the blood of Muslims, the Crusaders wept with joy as they thanked God in the Church of the Holy Sepulchre.

The Christian lords of the Holy Land

The map on page 47 shows you the lands which the Crusaders conquered, and how they set up their own rule, in defiance of the emperor at Constantinople, and in the face of all the power of the Muslims.

The Crusaders – that is, those who remained alive and who did not wish to return to western Europe – arranged things in their Kingdom of Jerusalem as they would have done in any feudal kingdom at home. Count Baldwin of Flanders took the title of king. Barons and knights held their lands on condition that they brought their men to fight for their lord. They built castles. Castles were even more necessary here than in Europe, and the Crusaders built some very strong ones indeed. Partly because they learned much from the skilled engineers of the Byzantine Greeks and from the Muslims, they built castles which were far better than anything known then in Europe.

Built on rock, with two concentric walls and huge projecting towers, Krak of the Knights was one of the most formidable crusader castles. It belonged to the order of St John.

You can see from the photograph the projecting towers from which the defenders could sweep the face of the wall with arrows; the rounded surfaces, from which missiles would glance without doing much damage; the 'concentric' plan, as it is called, of having two lines of walls and towers, the high ones just inside the low; the sheer massive strength of the buildings. All these ideas were to be copied in the castles of Europe, and you may spot some of them in pictures in other parts of this book. With so many enemies near them, the Crusaders needed every good idea that they could pick up.

You may have wondered why the castle in the picture is called Krak *of the Knights*. The reason is that it belonged to a special order of knights – the knights of the Hospital of St John of Jerusalem. They had taken the same sort of vow as monks, but served God by fighting the Muslims instead of by praying. As you may guess by the name, they began as pro-tectors of sick pilgrims, and to this day the Order of St John looks after ill and injured people. Even here, birth counted. The real knights had to be born members of the ruling class, but the sergeants, who ranked as squires, and the ordinary brothers could be common people. There were also chaplains to conduct the services of the order.

There were other famous orders of religious knights, such as the Templars, who took their name from the Temple of Jerusalem. Such orders were given lands in European kingdoms to help to pay for their war expenses, and sometimes built circular churches, the shape of the Church of the Holy Sepulchre in Jerusalem, on their estates. The picture opposite shows a round church built by the Hospitallers, and there is a famous Temple church in London. Among other orders were those who fought in the lands on the map on page 42. On the shore of the Baltic there were the Teutonic knights. The best-known Spanish order was that of Santiago, or St James, and the Portuguese had their Order of Christ. All these orders became rich and strong.

The men, knights and monks at the same time, were descri-bed by St Bernard, an important abbot and scholar who lived

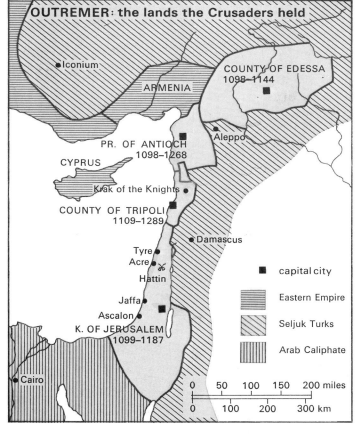

OUTREMER: the lands the Crusaders held

COUNTY OF EDESSA
1098–1144

ARMENIA

PR. OF ANTIOCH
1098–1268

CYPRUS

Krak of the Knights

COUNTY OF TRIPOLI
1109–1289

Tyre
Acre
Hattin

Jaffa

Ascalon

K. OF JERUSALEM
1099–1187

Iconium

Aleppo

Damascus

Cairo

■ capital city

Eastern Empire

Seljuk Turks

Arab Caliphate

0   50   100   150   200 miles
0   100   200   300 km

Little Maplestead Church, Essex. There have been
slight alterations since this nineteenth-century view
was engraved.

in the twelfth century: they 'never dress gaily and wash but
seldom. Shaggy by reason of their uncombed hair, they are
begrimed with dust, and swarthy from the weight of their
armour and the heat of the sun. They do their utmost to
possess strong and swift horses, but their mounts are not
garnished with ornaments or decked with trappings, for they
think of battle and victory, not of pomp and show. Such hath
God chosen for his own, who vigorously and faithfully guard
the Holy Sepulchre, all armed with the sword, and most
learned in the art of war.' They were the foremost fighters
among the Crusaders. In the two centuries of its existence, the
Order of the Temple had twenty-two Grand Masters, and
half of them died at the hands of the Muslims. When taken
prisoner, they were killed immediately, for they would

never change their religion and they would never pay ransom.

The orders of monk-knights in their castles were a force of
warriors always ready and anxious to fight the infidels.
Many of the knights and barons who settled in the Holy
Land, however, soon became very different. They began to
learn the Arabic language, to dress in long robes and turbans,
to take baths often, to employ skilled Arab doctors, to exchange
visits and gifts with the Muslim lords who lived across the
frontier, and even to intermarry with the local people. New
Crusaders, coming straight from Europe, where life was
much rougher, were shocked by what they considered to be the
softness and corruption of the lords settled in the Holy Land.
Of course, to anybody used to the civilisation of the Arabs,
the new arrivals seemed crude, brutal and rather stupid.

47

Order of Christ founded 1319 with former Templar lands (Portugal)

Order of Santiago c. 1161 (Castile)

Order of Teutonic Knights c. 1191

Order of the Temple c. 1118

Order of the Hospital of St. John of Jerusalem c. 1099

It is hard to say which sort of knight did more to keep safe the Crusader Kingdom of Jerusalem. Was it the skill and tact of those who had learnt to get on well with the Arab lords, or was it the warlike strength of the orders? Either way, if you look again at the map on page 47 you will wonder how the Crusaders were able to hang on to that narrow strip of land between the sea and the lands of Islam. The answer, most probably, lies not so much in the skill or strength of the Crusaders as in the constant quarrels among the Muslims, which prevented them from gathering all their power against the Kingdom of Jerusalem. So, for nearly a hundred years, the Christian lords from the West held their own.

The defeat of the Crusaders

Disaster came in 1187. There had arisen among the Muslims a man who was able to unite them. His name, as the Christians pronounced it, was Saladin. When he was ready, he waited until a Crusader lord broke the truce which had been signed between Saladin and the king of Jerusalem. This gave him the excuse he had been hoping for. He attacked with a large army. The king of Jerusalem gathered all his knights and lords. In the withering heat of a July day he led them into a rocky waste, where they were trapped, tired and without water. Almost all of them were killed or captured by Saladin.

Without enough men to defend them, and with no hope of a new army to relieve them, the castles and towns fell quickly. Jerusalem itself surrendered on 2 October 1187. Saladin forbade looting and destruction. He allowed Christians to go free, and to take their belongings with them, if they paid ransom. Many of the poorer Christians, however, could not afford the ransom, and were therefore taken as slaves; though rich Christians, including the bishop himself, were carrying away great quantities of money. Saladin and some of his men were so moved to pity that they freed, without ransom, thousands of their new slaves.

By acting like this, Saladin earned a reputation for being an honourable and generous man. He was trusted and respected by Christians as well as by his own men. So people were not afraid of what might happen if they surrendered to him, for he kept his promises.

Crosses and foundation dates of some of the most famous orders of crusading knights.

THE THIRD CRUSADE. All of the Holy Land fell into Saladin's hands except for one seaport, the ancient city of Tyre. The news came as a fearful shock in Western Christendom. Knights, lords and kings were filled with a fierce determination that the Holy Land must be rescued, at any cost. Crusaders began to stream eastwards. The Holy Roman Emperor himself, the ruler of the Germans and the senior among all the kings of the West came in person. He was a famous old warrior called Frederick Barbarossa, or Red-Beard. Unfortunately, he was accidentally drowned on the way; had he lived, he might have prevented the arguments between the other leaders of this Crusade. Two other powerful kings came with big armies; King Philip Augustus of France and King Richard Lionheart of England. They set about the reconquest of the Holy Land by laying siege to the strong port of Acre.

The story of King Richard's Crusade is very well known, and you must have heard it already. You will know that he was a great fighter, that he took Acre in 1191 and many other towns. Yet the Crusade collapsed before it could take Jerusalem. Saladin won. The Christians, with the sea and their ships behind them, were able to cling to their ports and

The Horns of Hattin, barren waterless hills between the fertile plain and the Sea of Galilee. Here the army of the Kingdom of Jerusalem was destroyed by Saladin in 1187.

coastal castles, but the rest of the Holy Land remained in the hands of the Muslims.

THE LATER CRUSADES. We know now that, after the failure of the great effort of the 1190s, the Crusaders had lost. But then they could not tell that the struggle was hopeless. One more effort, it seemed, might bring them to Jerusalem. There were many more Crusades, but something always went wrong.

There was a Crusade which, under the influence of the Venetians, ended in 1204 by taking Constantinople. The Crusaders held it until 1261, when the Greeks finally drove them out. So for more than half a century Western and Eastern Christians were fighting instead of helping each other.

There was the pathetic Children's Crusade of 1212. Thousands of children got the idea that God would give to them what he denied to proud and greedy lords; He would work a miracle for them. They marched from their homes in the

49

Emperor
Frederick
Barbarossa

King Philip
Augustus

King Richard
Lionheart

The leaders
of the Third Crusade,
as represented
on their seals.

middle of Germany and France to the Mediterranean Sea, but the sea did not open in front of them. Worn out by their journey, most of them never reached home again. Unhappiest of all were those taken aboard ship by merchants who promised to carry them to the Holy Land; instead, the merchants took them to Africa and sold them as slaves.

There were times of truce. From 1229 to 1244 the Holy Roman Emperor Frederick II was allowed by the Muslims to be king of Jerusalem. There were times of serious fighting, as when St Louis, king of France, attacked Egypt in 1260. He chose Egypt because it was the strongest of the Muslim lands, and if he could win here the rest would be fairly easy. But Egypt was so strong that Louis was taken prisoner, and his ransom cost France 800,000 pieces of gold.

The end came in 1291, when the Christians lost Acre. It was just a hundred years after it had been taken by the Third Crusade.

The Mongols and their empire

Towards the end of the time of the Crusades there had been one real chance that the Muslims might be overwhelmed, though not by the power of the Crusaders alone.

About the time of Saladin, another great conqueror was at work, far to the east in central Asia, among the wild nomadic tribes who had so often swept out of their steppes upon the farms and cities of more civilised peoples. This man was called Temujin, but he is better known by the title he won: Jenghiz Khan, or Mightiest King.

The map shows what he did. He was able to make himself the leader of all the Mongol tribes. You know what they could do, if you remember the Huns, or the Magyars, or the Seljuk Turks. Jenghiz Khan wanted to do more than earlier nomad leaders. He divided his followers into armies called 'urdus'; this is our word 'horde'. As you see, he gave the hordes different duties. Within the lands he had taken, he enforced order. Across the plains and deserts his messengers galloped, changing horses at regular post-stations, while the camel caravans shambled slowly along the tracks. Any tribesmen who interfered would have to face the vengeance of the Great Khan. Temujin died in 1227, but for many years the empire was held together by his sons and grandsons, who followed one who was recognised as the Great Khan.

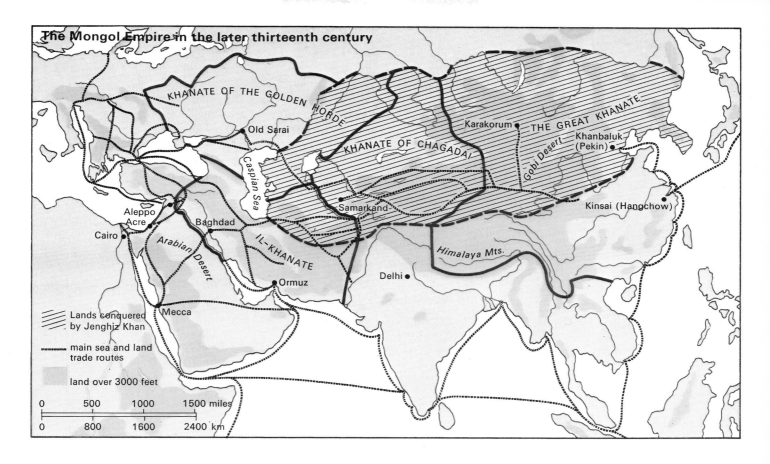

The Mongol Empire in the later thirteenth century

KHANATE OF THE GOLDEN HORDE

Old Sarai

Caspian Sea

Karakorum · THE GREAT KHANATE

KHANATE OF CHAGADAI

Gobi Desert

Khanbaluk (Pekin)

Aleppo
Acre

Cairo

Arabian Desert

Baghdad

IL-KHANATE

Samarkand

Kinsai (Hangchow)

Himalaya Mts.

Ormuz

Delhi

Mecca

Lands conquered by Jenghiz Khan

main sea and land trade routes

land over 3000 feet

| 0 | 500 | 1000 | 1500 miles |
| 0 | 800 | 1600 | 2400 km |

Under the Great Khan, the other khans went on with their conquests. From China to Russia, no forces could defeat the hordes of Mongol horse-archers.

What gave hope to some of the Crusaders was the discovery that some of these Mongols were Christians. They were tribes which had been converted hundreds of years before by wandering missionaries, and they did not look to either Rome or Constantinople for guidance, but they were certainly Christians of a sort. Besides, even those who were not Christian did not seem to be enemies of the Church, and they were doing terrible damage to the Muslims. Therefore the Pope and some of the kings of Europe sent messengers to the Great Khan, suggesting that he should join them in an attack on the Muslims.

It came to nothing. The Great Khan was polite, but he had other things to think about, and he did not need help from Crusaders.

All the same, in 1258, some of the Mongols struck the Muslims a mighty blow. They attacked Baghdad, city of the caliphs and most splendid centre of civilisation in all Islam. They destroyed it completely, and Muslim civilisation was never the same again. Yet the Mongols did not push on much further. The great empire was slowly beginning to fall apart, each piece under its own khan. Egypt held firm, and the Holy Land was never restored to the Christians.

What the Crusades did

The Crusades were one of the most famous struggles in history. What had they done, in the end? The Spaniards and Portuguese and the Teutonic knights succeeded, but these were not the main Crusades. It may well be that the main Crusades did little else than make Christians and Muslims much more bitter enemies than they had been before.

Some Christian doctors may have learned from the more skilled Arab doctors. Christian soldiers picked up new ideas about building and taking castles. Warriors, pilgrims, messengers to the Great Khan, all learned more about the world and the people who lived in it, though it is difficult to see what use they made of this knowledge.

The people who probably gained most from the Crusades were the merchants, not the men of religion nor the men of war. Traders from Italian cities like Genoa, Venice and Pisa made money by carrying soldiers over the sea, and became richer still through trading in the silks and spices which came from the Far East to the cities of the Near East.

A good deal of this might just as easily have happened if there had never been any Holy Wars, and anyway these results seem little when we look at what they cost. The Byzantine Empire had been fatally hurt, as much by the Crusaders as by the Muslims. Baghdad, the old great home of Muslim culture, lay in ruins, though this was not the work of the Crusaders. Thousands of people had fought and died like heroes and martyrs, on both sides, in a struggle that has never been forgotten. But it seems to have been a struggle that settled nothing.

Chivalry

During the time of the Crusades the word 'knight' came to mean something more than 'armoured horseman' or 'lord of the manor'. It came to mean a man who tried to use his strength and wealth in doing good for those who were weaker and poorer. The new idea was that a true knight was not only faithful to his lord, but should also protect churchmen, serve ladies, be kind to the unfortunate. He should always be brave and courteous. He should never be boastful or greedy or aggressive or drunken, but quiet and modest. This idea of how a knight ought to behave was called 'chivalry'

the bad knight

the good knight

A chivalrous knight was a very different sort of man from the proud, unruly, land-grabbing, brutal warriors who seem to have been only too common in the Middle Ages. Did such warriors turn into chivalrous knights? Or was chivalry only a game of make-believe, a fashionable game which the ruling classes played when they were not busy quarrelling and scheming for more land, or following their lords to war, or trying to squeeze more out of the peasants and merchants who lived on their land? Were these people 'bold bad barons' or were they 'very perfect gentle knights'? Or were they very mixed? You need to read about some of the most important kings and lords of the Middle Ages before you make up your mind.

Certainly, boys of the ruling class were supposed to be brought up to be good knights. Their parents sent them to the castles of other lords. Here they would begin as pages to the ladies, who would teach them good manners and gentle behaviour. Then they would become squires, acting as servants to knights and thus learning about armour, weapons and horses. The chaplain of the castle would see that they were religious, while the lord of the castle would watch over their progress generally. When a squire was old enough and had shown that he was good enough, the lord would make him a knight. Sometimes a man would be knighted for great valour on the battlefield, but more often it was as you see in the sketch.

faults. Yet, though there was a rule that only tried and tested knights could be members, the duke's son in 1433 was made a knight of the order when he was twenty days old. That boy grew up to be Duke Charles the Bold, and he thought little of massacring the people of towns he captured; though he usually spared the churches.

The Church also tried to reduce the feuding, robbing and killing by 'the Truce of God'. This meant that no man should fight his enemy on certain days of the week. The Church tried

page   squire   knight

It was an honour to be made a knight, to be called 'Sir' and to wear a knightly sword and spurs. Soon after the end of the Crusades, some kings thought of making some knights more highly honoured still. They set up orders of knighthood, and the members were supposed to be specially brave and good. These orders were not like those of the Templars and Hospitallers, but more like clubs which a knight could join only if the king invited him. Many of these orders exist to this day; for example, the Knights of the Garter in Britain. The order was founded by Edward III about 1349. The knights wear the badge of St George, and carry on an old-fashioned garter their motto, which means, 'Evil be to him who evil thinks.' Another very famous order was that of the Golden Fleece, founded by the duke of Burgundy in 1429 'for the reverence of God and the sustenance of our Christian faith, and to honour and enhance the noble order of chivalry'. Each year the knights were to meet in a Chapter and, with feasts and religious services, discuss one another's conduct during the past twelve months, praising those who had done well and blaming those who had not acted as good knights ought. Sometimes it went like that, even the duke of Burgundy himself being rebuked for his

to enforce the Truce of God, but had to give up in the end, for it never was properly respected. The Church also said that it was wicked to fight simply for pay, because a Christian should fight only when he believed that it was right to do so. Therefore, all mercenaries were to be excommunicated; but men still went on selling their swords to the highest bidder. The Church tried to make war less horrible by forbidding crossbows to be used, except against heathens; since they were good weapons soldiers went on using them.

From all this, you could argue that the Church had failed in its efforts to improve the feudal ruling class; but that would not be the whole truth. You must remember that, whatever they sometimes did, there had been thousands of barons and knights who had gone to the Crusades without any intention of becoming lords in the Holy Land and who, if they survived, had been content to return home poorer than when they had left. And, even if they did not always live up to it, knights believed in the ideal of chivalry as something which they should try to follow. Men who believed and sometimes acted thus were different from their ancestors who had led the barbarian invasions or the Viking raids.

4. The ordinary people

The third estate

So far in this book we have been considering the two important classes, or estates, of people in the Middle Ages; the churchmen who ruled men's minds and consciences; the kings and barons and knights who were masters of everything else.

Though they were so powerful, the Church and the ruling class were very small. If you had been born in the Middle Ages, the chances are strongly against your having been anything but a poor villager. We do not know the chances exactly, because there was no census and so there are no figures of population, but we are quite sure that most people lived in the country. Some lived on scattered hill farms, but most were in villages. Towns grew bigger as time went on, but even at the end of the Middle Ages something like 80 per cent or 90 per cent of the people were villagers.

Townsmen and countrymen alike, ordinary people were all part of this third estate. Life in village and town was very different, though. As most people were villagers, we shall begin with them.

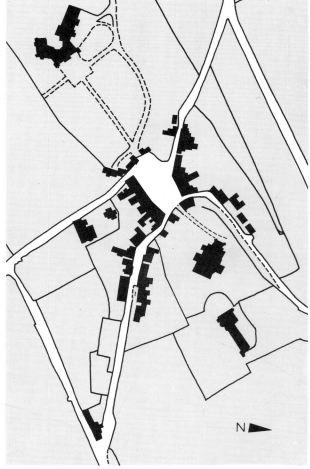

Chilham, Kent (*left*), remains a small cluster of cottages between the castle (just visible at the top left of the photograph) and the church.

Clare, Suffolk (*below*), has become a small town. The church is in the centre and the castle motte can be seen to the south-east.

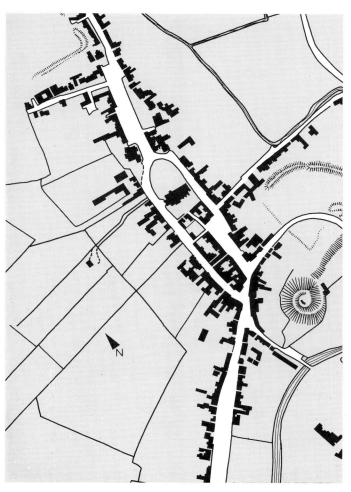

The life of a villager

You have already read something about how a village was ruled. Here, to remind you, are two English villages. One is small and the other has grown into a small country town, but each shows very clearly the two important buildings; the church and the castle. On pages 6 and 32 you learned of the priest and the lord of the manor, who used those buildings. The ordinary villagers used the cottages.

A cottage would be big enough to hold a peasant and his family, and sometimes his animals. There are not many English cottages which go right back to the Middle Ages, but until fairly recently some people in Scotland and Ireland lived in houses like those shown overleaf. Notice that they are built from whatever materials could most easily be found in that part of the countryside. In England wood and clay and straw were

The cottage on the left, at Didbrook, Gloucestershire, clearly shows the big Λ-shaped timbers, called crucks, which support the whole frame.

The thatchers are at Long Compton, Warwickshire. There is little wood to be seen about the Irish cottage in County Kerry, and the fuel piled in the foreground is peat.

often the easiest to get, and English cottages would be built as these photographs show. There would be a strong frame of wood, which was the skeleton of the house. The roof would frequently be made of straw or reed thatch, though sometimes strips of thin wood were used. The spaces left in the walls between the main timbers were filled with basket-work covered by clay or plaster; this was called 'wattle and daub'. Houses like this were fairly simple to build and mend. Even if the cottager himself could not do everything, there was nothing that would be too difficult for some village workman.

Inside the cottage there would be space to eat and sleep, and probably no more. Furniture – a table and a few stools – would be strong and simple, the sort that a village carpenter could make. Beds were the same; up to the fifteenth century it seems that some peasants were using blocks of wood as pillows. Sometimes there may have been only one room in the cottage, but sometimes there may have been an attic in the roof for sleeping, and even an extra room on the ground.

Cooking would be done over the fire, which usually lacked a chimney, in pots of earthenware or, if the peasant was lucky, metal. Such cooking utensils might be too much for a village craftsman to make, and would be bought at the nearest market. Plates would be merely flat pieces of wood, and cutlery would be the peasant's ordinary working knife, with a wooden or horn spoon.

Clothes would be just as simple, often made from wool which had been spun into thread by the women and children, and sometimes woven locally. Some cloth and leather, though, would probably have to be bought at the market, in the nearest town.

On every day except holy-days and Sundays, the peasant would be at work in the fields, unless he had to go to market or attend the manor court, or unless he had some special village job, such as finding stray animals and putting them in the village pound until the owner paid a fine for them.

The pictures on the next pages will give you some idea of the

above: A Highland 'black house' on the island of Lewis. Outside it is low-built against the winter storms, with the thatch held down by weighted ropes. Inside it may be smoky, but it is snug.

below: Knives, pewter spoons and wooden bowls of the later Middle Ages. Though found in London, they are typical of what ordinary people everywhere probably used. The knives are 9 inches (23 cm) long.

Longthorpe Tower, Peterborough. The tower itself is a fourteenth-century addition to a somewhat earlier hall, and is famous for the paintings on the wall of its main room. Those shown here are: in the centre, the Nativity; above, the Seven Ages of Man — a baby in its cradle, a boy with ball and whip, a youth, a man with his hawk, a middle-aged man, an old man with a moneybag, and a very aged man hobbling with two sticks: below is a frieze of the Apostles, and below that a frieze of birds from the nearby fens.

work that went on, all the year round. For most people, this was the whole of their life. The fields were the same sort of huge open areas, divided into strips like long allotments, as the open fields of the time of the Anglo-Saxons and Franks. As you saw on page 32, most peasants were not allowed to leave their work, though their lord could not take their share of the fields away from them; and they paid the lord for his protection by working on his strips of field as well as their own.

Were the villagers happy or contented? We have no way of telling, for nobody in those days bothered to write down much about them and they themselves could not write. The work was hard, no doubt, but it was in the open air, they were used to it and, except at times like harvest, they did not have to hurry. Their 'rest' days probably came to a good total every year, when all the various festivals and holy-days were reckoned up. They had their rights: in the manor court they advised the lord about what needed doing, and what the customs of the manor were. Even if they were not happy, there was little that they could do about it. When life became too miserable to be endured, or when something happened to whip up annoyance and frustration into anger, there might be a peasant revolt. Such revolts, though, like the French Jacquerie in 1358 and the English Peasants' Revolt of 1381, were almost certain to end in disaster.

If you were born a peasant, you usually remained a peasant. Perhaps, if you were a clever boy, your lord might let you go to be a churchman. Or you might be allowed to be a soldier, or a servant of the lord. A very clever and lucky peasant might even rise to the rank of knight. That did not often happen, but these pictures show you a house which belonged to a man whose grandfather had been a serf. His family rose by managing the lands of the abbot of Peterborough.

Most villagers were serfs, that is, unfree. Other people looked down on villagers. The word for a man who lived in a 'vill' or village was 'villein', and you know what it means, spelled 'villain', nowadays. In spite of this, the villeins themselves seem gradually to have been able to make themselves free, often by buying their liberty. This happened as money became more common, and goods were bought and sold for coins, instead of being bartered. That led to two things; first, peasants could save up money in a way that was impossible with, say, grain and vegetables and eggs, and hide it away until they had a reasonable amount; second, the lords

above: Different agricultural tasks, shown in a diorama in the Science Museum, London. At the right is part of the evidence for the reconstruction, a picture from the fourteenth-century Luttrell Psalter.

left: A deserted medieval village site at Cowlam, Yorkshire. The shadows reveal the pronounced hollow of the main street, the low banks separating the villagers' tofts, and the position of some cottages.

often found it more convenient to be paid rents in money rather than in work or in farm produce. So, on some manors, peasants would agree with the lord to pay him so much money a year, instead of working for him. Villagers without land became labourers, working for money. This sort of thing seems to have happened more often as centuries went on.

Whether they remained serfs or not, most people remained peasants or labourers until the end of the Middle Ages, and for long afterwards.

overleaf: In the fifteenth century the Duke of Berry had a Book of Hours so magnificently illuminated that it is called *The Very Rich Hours.* Each month has its picture. Here we see the February landscape and the scene outside one of the Duke's castles, Poitiers, in July.

Townsmen—the craftsmen make

The simple idea about society in the Middle Ages is this: the priests prayed, the knights fought, the peasants worked, and everyone knew his place. Though that is roughly a true picture of medieval life, it is too rough. There is no room in it for people who lived by making things and selling them, the men of the towns. In villages there were carpenters and smiths, in castles there were skilled workers in leather and metal, and in monasteries there were writers and illustrators of books. Up to a point, villages and castles and monasteries had their own craftsmen. But this was not enough.

If you look at some of the pictures in this book, you will see buildings which do not look as though they were designed or built by local craftsmen, but by men who had years of training and experience in that sort of work. Or take the example (page 65) of the tomb of Edward, the Black Prince, in Canterbury cathedral. Look carefully at the statue itself, at the painting, at the leather-work and metal-work of shield, helmet, spurs, belt. Only highly skilled craftsmen could do these. Of course, as the son of King Edward III, the Black Prince was the second greatest man in England, and nothing but the very best would do for him. But we use him as an example because so much happens to be left on his tomb. You may find splendid tombs and brasses in many churches and cathedrals in Europe and all these men wanted really good armour and clothes, and tapestries on their walls and cups on their tables and jewels round their necks, as well as expensive tombs. Their wives, too, probably expected to be equally well clothed and housed. Churches, too, demanded beautiful and precious vestments and vessels, like these on the next pages. Although such articles may be luxuries, think of the number of great lords and rich churches there were to buy them.

Besides, there were goods of high quality which would be bought by anyone who could afford them. Shoes and boots of properly tanned, supple leather, which would really fit; knives of good iron, which would really cut; well-made pots and pans, buckles and bowstrings were all well worth having. So, even when most people lived a simple, poor life, there was a need for skilled craftsmen; and the more people came to have a little money to spare, the more they would spend on properly made articles like these.

The cupboard is 3 feet (91 cm) high. On it stand two decorated earthenware pitchers, a bronze cauldron and an iron flesh-hook, used in kitchens to examine food being stewed.

Table jugs. The horse, from which the rider has been broken, was the kind used in rinsing hands before forks were introduced. It is 14 inches (36 cm) long.

All these articles were found in London, and date from the fourteenth and fifteenth centuries.

Even in the more backward north and west of Europe it was natural for craftsmen to settle where there were good markets, and for towns to grow. In many places, especially the south of Europe, cities had survived since Roman times, but in other places they had died during the barbarian invasions, and had to begin all over again. In medieval towns it was quite usual for men of the same craft to live in the same street. You may know of places where streets still have such names as Silver Street or Butcher Bank. This picture is of a street still called the Shambles, which means a slaughter-house or a place where meat is sold. The street itself has hardly changed since the Middle Ages, though it is no longer full of butchers' shops.

Sometimes a town or a country would be especially famous for one product. Perhaps this would be caused by some goodness in the earth or water there, or perhaps it would be that the men of a certain craft were very skilful. Cordova leather-work was so famous that in England leather-workers were called 'cordwainers'. If he could afford it, a medieval knight might want a sword from Toledo or Passau, and armour from Milan or Augsburg; he might prefer to drink wine from Gascony or Cyprus, and dress in cloth made by Flemish weavers from English wool. He might keep jewels in a box enamelled at Limoges, and decorate the chapel of his castle with alabaster carved in Nottingham and stained glass from York.

Sometimes there were very expensive luxuries from far away, like the silk from China or the furs from Russia, or Eastern spices to make food more tasty and to help in preserving it. Spices were for the rich, but everyone needed salt, and that sometimes had to be brought from a distance. Since there was no refrigeration salt was the main means of preserving meat and fish, and during times like Lent, when the Church ordered people to do without meat, there was a big demand for salt fish.

left: Bronze lantern, showing the candle-holder and the fittings for the horn window, now missing. It is 6 inches (15 cm) high.

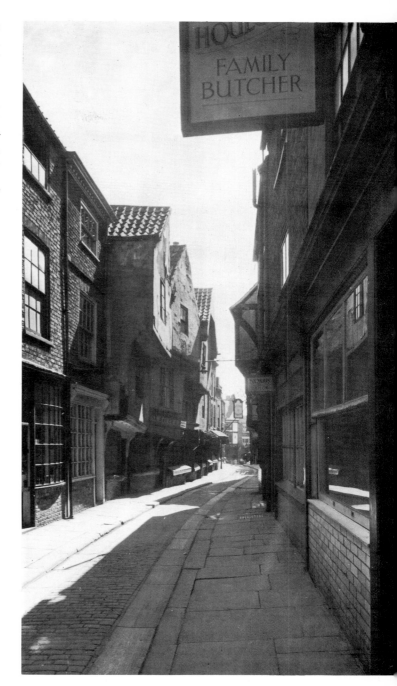

The Shambles, York.

MEDIEVAL CRAFTSMANSHIP

Mitre of St Thomas Becket, English embroidery, late twelfth century. It has lost its enamelled and jewelled ornaments.

Chasuble, made in England about 1400–30. The silk probably came from Italy.

right: Armour made for the Elector Frederick I of the Rhenish Palatinate by Tomaso da Missaglia of Milan, about 1445.

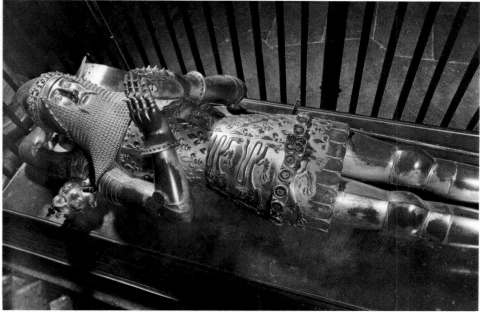

above left: The Black Prince's funeral achievements, 1376: shield, tabard, helm with cap of maintenance. These are replicas which show how bright the originals were when new.

left: Late fifteenth-century English carving in alabaster. It shows a miracle of St Edmund, and comes from a set intended to decorate an altar. It is 15½ inches (39·3 cm) high.

right: Ewer of gilt bronze, enriched with silver, made in the Meuse region, mid-twelfth century. It stands 8¼ inches (21 cm) high.

above: Bronze effigy of the Black Prince, on his tomb in Canterbury Cathedral. The funeral achievements hang above it.

Townsmen – the merchants deal

All these things meant trade, and trade meant merchants. Some merchants travelled only a few score miles around their homes, but others went hundreds. Some even ventured through the lands of the Great Khan, to China. Merchants carried goods by water when they could, which was cheaper and often faster than the trains of pack-animals and the camel caravans which had usually to be used on land, for lack of good roads.

Merchants did their trading at markets and at fairs. Markets were usually small-scale affairs, held regularly. They would happen once, or perhaps more often, per week for the people of the district. Most towns in Europe still have their weekly market-days. This one is fairly typical of the market in an English county town. Notice how the river, the bridge and the parish church are close together; the castle, too, used to stand close by. Fairs were much bigger than markets, and happened only two or three times a year. More merchants came, and from far away. Some fairs were famous for trading in certain goods, like those of Ypres and other Flemish towns for cloth. Most big fairs, however, brought together merchants who wished to sell and to buy all sorts of goods.

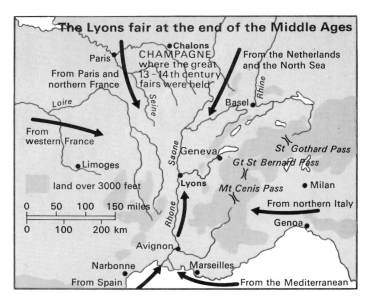

Bedford still clearly shows how it grew. Traffic converges on the bridge. Beside is the market, with church on one side and tree-fringed castle motte on the other.

Towns grow

Soon we shall have to look more carefully at how some of the trading was carried on, but for the moment all we need to understand is that there was plenty of work for craftsmen and merchants, and it was only common sense for them to come together in those places which were most suitable for their work. So, as trade increased, towns grew.

Usually, if we look at any town which grew up during the Middle Ages, we see that there were good reasons. The diagram sums it up: water transport plus land transport. If a bridge were built, it would prevent ships from sailing further up-stream, so they would have to unload at the town. Further-more, there were not very many bridges over big rivers, so traffic converged there. Then there was the question of safety. If the king or a strong lord had a castle there, and seemed ready to protect the lives and goods of people who settled near by, that was a great advantage for craftsmen and merchants who had to keep valuables. This was to the advantage of the lord, too, for the townsmen would be willing to pay for his protection. The richer the town became, the more he should be able to get out of them. At last the town would become rich enough to afford a good wall of its own. The lord of the town would have to give permission for a market or fair to be held, and he would be able to collect fees from it.

food and raw materials come in from the countryside

finished goods are sold at market or in shops

market place

protecting castle

ships can come up river, but must unload at bridge

merchants can cross the river

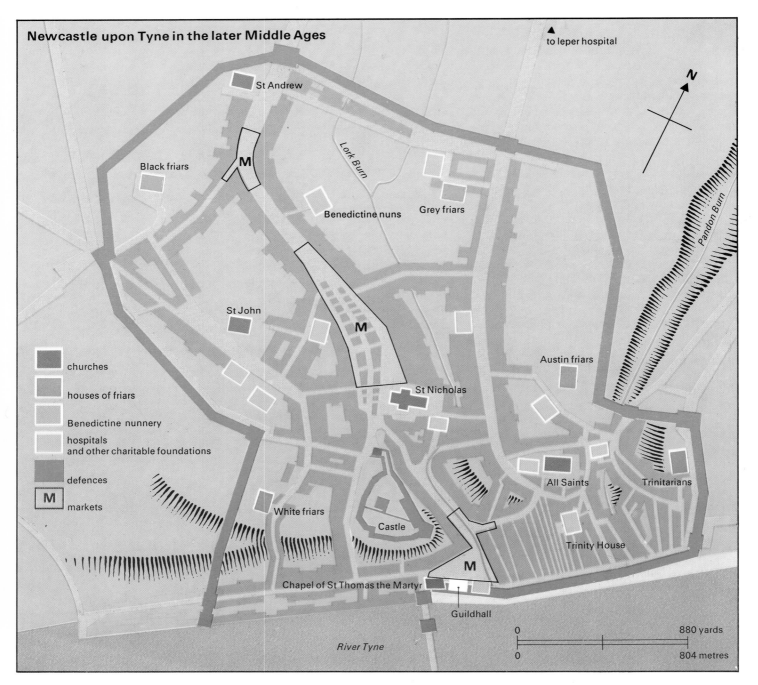

Newcastle upon Tyne in the later Middle Ages

to leper hospital

N

St Andrew

Lork Burn

M

Black friars

Benedictine nuns

Grey friars

Pandon Burn

St John

M

Austin friars

St Nicholas

churches

houses of friars

Benedictine nunnery

hospitals
and other charitable foundations

defences

M markets

White friars

All Saints

Trinitarians

Castle

Trinity House

M

Chapel of St Thomas the Martyr

Guildhall

0   880 yards

0   804 metres

River Tyne

The lantern shining from the tower of St Nicholas, Newcastle upon Tyne.

Often, even in a great modern city, it is easy to see how the place took shape in the Middle Ages. Newcastle upon Tyne is a good example; even the name gives two of the reasons why there is a town there. Look at the map opposite of the town as it was at the end of the Middle Ages. You can see here on the ground all the features of the diagram on page 67. You can also see how the town grew outwards, from the castle and main church and markets, along the roads to the north, east and west. There was difficulty caused by the narrow but deep gorge of the Lork Burn, which had been an excellent defence for one side of the castle, but which was a serious obstacle to traders as well as enemies. This explains why the town grew more on one side than on the other, and why, when the walls were built, they had to enclose such an oddly shaped town.

There are one or two other things which you may notice about this medieval town. The friars were strong here, for this was just the sort of centre they wanted. There were hospitals. The churches were beautified by rich townsmen; this famous tower was paid for by one Robert Rhodes in the middle of the fifteenth century. Notice that it is not only beautiful and unusual, but that it is also a fine piece of engineering. It was useful, too, for a lantern at the top showed the way to be-nighted travellers by road and river.

The town plan also shows a Guildhall. To the merchants of any flourishing town, their Guildhall was of the utmost importance. In the next section of the book we shall see why.

below: Probably the finest of all market crosses, built by Bishop Story of Chichester in 1501 at the central crossroads of the city.

Townsmen look after their own

Merchants and craftsmen, especially merchants, were men whose jobs were very much concerned with money. Since they often had a lot, other people sometimes felt like taking some of it from them. The lord of the town might be short of money, and he might expect the merchants to help him; and he had ways of making it awkward for them if they did not feel generous. Robbers often infested the more lonely roads; when Edward I of England ordered that trees and bushes should be cleared for a bowshot on each side of main roads, he had a sound reason. Even when a merchant reached another town he was not safe; some merchant of this town might allege that he owed him money, and even if the accusation was false the accused man would be at a disadvantage if it was only his word against that of his accuser.

To defend themselves, the merchants first had to agree to forming a union or guild which would come to the help of any member in trouble. Such a union, to which all the merchants of the town belonged, whatever goods they bought and sold, was called a Merchant Guild.

The Merchant Guild made sure that nobody in the town let it down. Any merchant who would not join and loyally do what the guild ordered was forced to leave the town. After this, the guild was in a position to bargain with the lord of the town. Sometimes the lord would be none other than the king himself, and this would be lucky, for the king would be just as much in need of extra money as any other lord – often more so – and he was able to give more privileges in return.

The guildsmen would ask their lord for permission to look after various things for themselves, instead of leaving the entire running of the town to the lord's bailiff. Take the market as an example. At first, the bailiff would collect all the fees from the merchants who came, and judge all disputes, and take the fines of people who had misbehaved. The Merchant Guild would ask if it could do this. If the guild had chosen a good time, when the lord was in a pleasant mood and yet wanted some extra money, and if they offered enough, the

The perils of a merchant's life:
1 at home, extortion by the lord;
2 on the road, robbery;
3 in strange towns, fraud and false witness.

70

lord would have a parchment document written for them, and put his seal on it, allowing what they asked. Such a document was called a charter. The guild would take this charter and lock it up carefully, perhaps in a strong chest in their Guildhall, for this was their guarantee.

As years went on, the guild would try to get more charters out of the lord, until at last they had permission to run almost everything in the town. So they would ask if they could appoint their own men to govern the town instead of the lord's bailiff. They would call their officials the mayor and aldermen. Thus, by getting a final big charter and usually by paying the lord a fixed rent every year, the Merchant Guild of many a town came to be able to rule the town as it pleased.

Some English towns were even able to get from the king permission to appoint their own sheriffs, and to be classed as counties, though only a few of the richest – London, York, Bristol and Newcastle – managed this.

In the Guildhall, besides their precious charters, the mayor and the other great men of the town sat in council and held their courts, jealously guarding the privileges they had won.

Towns which were as strong and rich as this were able and willing to help the king to keep law and order in his kingdom. At first, it is true, many towns preferred to rely on their own strength, especially if they were able to join up with other towns to form a league. In England some of the main seaports of the south-east, the Cinque (Five) Ports, did this, and were able to persuade the king to allow them special privileges in return for supplying him with ships. These men had no hesitation in taking stern action if they thought that some other sailors were interfering with their trade, and there were fierce fights between ships of the Cinque Ports and of their main rival, Yarmouth, during the thirteenth century. Such disorder was always worse at sea than on land; at sea it was easy to dispose of any unwanted ships and sailors. Piracy was easy, and even in 'correct' warfare prisoners were not taken in sea-fights. Despite their readiness to take care of themselves, however, merchants fought only when they had to, to protect their trade. Therefore, if a king showed that he was strong enough to have a chance of keeping the peace, he could usually rely on the backing of the towns in his kingdom. This happened, as you will see, in England, France and Spain where strong kingdoms were made, but not in Italy, Germany and the Netherlands.

HENRY, KING OF ENGLAND, Duke of Normandy and Aquitaine, and Count of Anjou, To his Archbishops, Bishops, Abbots, Earls, Barons, Justiciaries, Sheriffs, Ministers and all his faithful subjects of England and Normandy, GREETING.
KNOW YE that I have granted to my citizens of York all their liberties, laws and customs and by name their Gild of Merchants and Hanses, in England and Normandy, and their Lastages throughout all the coasts of the sea, quit as they ever most freely and best had them in the time of King Henry my grandfather.
AND I WILL and firmly command that they have and hold the aforesaid liberties and customs, with all the liberties belonging to their aforesaid Gild and to their Hanses, as well and as peaceably and as freely and quietly as ever they best, most freely and most quietly, had and held them in the time of the aforesaid King Henry my grandfather.
Witnesses, Roger, Archbishop of York, and Thomas, Chancellor, and Reginald, Earl of Cornwall, and Warren Fitz Henry, Chamberlain, at Westminster.

Protection for merchants: the town charter. This one was granted by Henry II between 1155 and 1162 to the men of York.

The great merchant cities of Europe

The three countries which we mentioned last were all supposed to be parts of the Holy Roman Emperor's lands, though Germany was the centre of the empire. The emperor had too hard a task, trying to enforce law and order over such a wide area. His authority was challenged by the great lords and barons on one side, and the Pope on the other, because both the barons and the Pope feared that a powerful emperor would take away many of the rights and privileges which they enjoyed. In the end, the Holy Roman Emperor lost all his power in Italy and the Netherlands, and most of his power even in Germany. Because there was no alternative, the towns in those three countries had to look after themselves, unless they were willing to submit to a local count or duke.

In Italy some towns remained about the same size for most of the Middle Ages, like Assisi (page 25). Others grew so rich and strong that they were not only able to defend themselves against all attackers, but began to conquer other places themselves. Venice, safe on her islands behind a powerful navy, had helped the Crusaders to take Constantinople (page 49). Her share of the loot, eventually, was a chain of ports and forts and islands, which made voyages easier and safer for Venetian ships trading to the eastern Mediterranean. Florence, on the

The expansion of Venice 1200–1500

sea trade routes

0   100   200   300 miles

0   200   400 km

Milan

Venice

Genoa

Florence

Zara 1202

DALMATIA 1420

Danube

Rome

Cattaro 1420

Durazzo 1205 1392

Constantinople

CORFU 1215 1386

CEPHALONIA
1209 1375

NEGROPONTE
(Euboea)
1211 1383 (lost 1470)

Nauplia 1388
Modon 1206
Monemvasia 1460

NAXOS 1207 1494

Mediterranean Sea

CRETE 1212

Dates of acquisition are given; some places taken after the Fourth Crusade were given up but retaken later

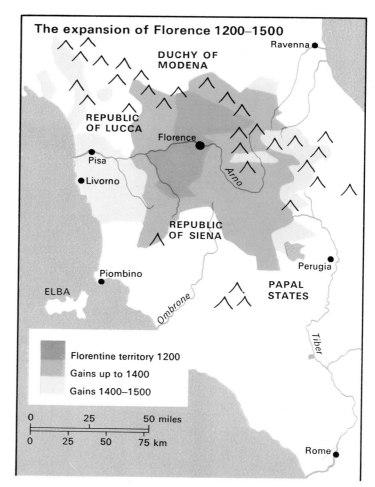

The expansion of Florence 1200–1500

Ravenna

DUCHY OF MODENA

REPUBLIC OF LUCCA

Florence

Pisa

Livorno

Arno

REPUBLIC OF SIENA

Perugia

Piombino

PAPAL STATES

ELBA

Ombrone

Tiber

Florentine territory 1200

Gains up to 1400

Gains 1400–1500

0   25   50 miles

0   25   50   75 km

Rome

other hand, did not spread her power over the sea, for her wealth depended more on wool than on trade with the East. Florence spread in Italy itself, taking near-by towns and cities, and was at last strong enough to take even the famous city of Pisa. In cities like Venice and Florence, the merchants held control firmly. The Guildhall of the Florentines has battle-ments, and they were not merely ornaments. The citizens of these merchant republics were ready to use force. Some great Italian cities, like Milan and Naples and Rome, remained under the rule of duke or king or Pope, though even here the citizens sometimes showed their rulers that it was safer to treat townsmen with respect.

Palazzo Vecchio (the Old Palace), built about 1300, was the seat of the government of the Republic of Florence. It was not unknown for rebels or conspirators against the state to be hanged or flung down from its windows.

In Venice the famous Bridge of Sighs was not built until 1597, to connect the Doge's Palace with the new prison. During the Middle Ages state prisoners were kept on the ground floor of the palace itself.

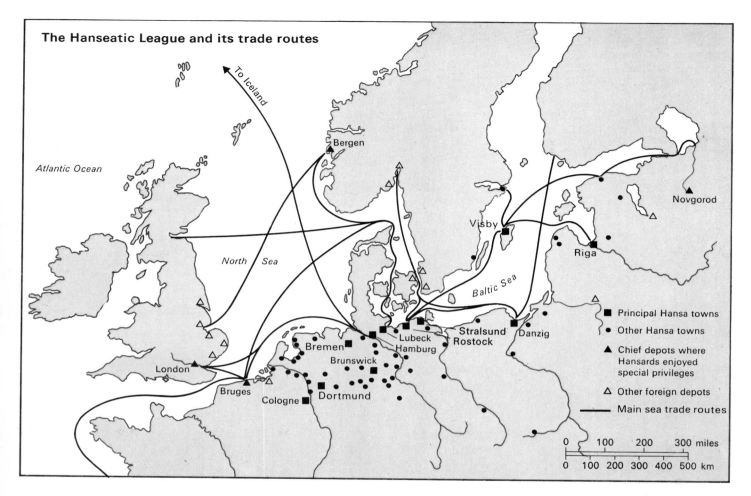

The Hanseatic League and its trade routes

It was very much the same with the cities of the Netherlands and Germany. Though the merchants sometimes were willing to accept their lord and to pay him great sums of money, they were also ready to fight for their rights. In Flanders, especially, there was always serious trouble if count or duke or bishop demanded too much of the men of his cities.

The most famous of all the leagues of merchant cities was the Hansa. The map shows the towns which were members, and the area which the Hansa covered. The Hanseatic merchants were masters of the Baltic Sea and its trade from about the middle of the thirteenth century until about the middle of the fifteenth century. During those two hundred years they

fought and beat anyone, from pirate to king, who resisted them. In many towns which did not belong to their league, the Hansards (as the merchants of the Hansa were called) had warehouses with special privileges. Their warehouse still stands in King's Lynn. In London they had charters from the kings of England which made their warehouses, the Steelyard, almost a little city on its own, and the merchants of the Steelyard had the right to elect one of the aldermen of the City of London. In England these merchants were called Easterlings, since they came from lands on the eastern side of the North Sea, and some people think that our modern word 'sterling' for a certain type of money comes from that name.

The Cloth Hall, Ypres, was one of the most spectacular monuments to the prosperity and pride of Low Countries townsmen in the thirteenth and fourteenth centuries. The photograph shows it before it was devastated in the First World War.

below: Hansa warehouses. The row of large ones stands by a quiet backwater in Lubeck, once the commercial centre of northern Europe. The smaller one is in King's Lynn, where the Hansards had a depot.

The trade routes

This map shows the great merchant cities which we have just mentioned, and several more. It explains why it was cities in these positions which became so important. One reason, as we saw on page 62, is that something valuable was grown or mined or made near those cities. The other main reason is: communications. These cities are placed where it is convenient for merchants to carry goods. A good example is the position of Venice and Genoa. They are so placed that goods from Asia can travel a great distance by water (remember what you learned on page 66) and are close to the passes over the Alps, which lead to the river routes through the centre of Europe.

The map shows the position in the later part of the Middle Ages, about 1400. The trade and the cities had taken many centuries to grow, but now the merchants and their money had become very important indeed. Both the Church and the feudal ruling class, whether they liked it or not, were having to rely more and more on the help of the men with the money.

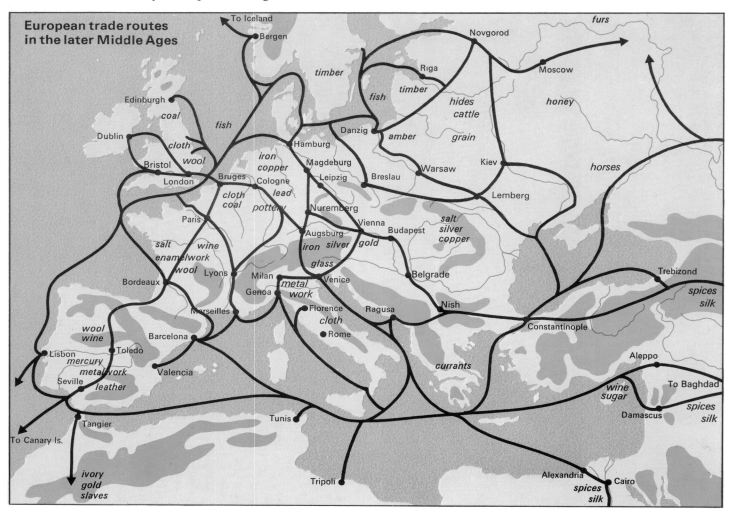

European trade routes in the later Middle Ages

Craft guilds and the fair price

So far we have been talking as if in every city there was only one Merchant Guild, which ran everything and to which all the merchants and craftsmen belonged. This is not the full truth. Besides the Merchant Guild, there often grew up special guilds for the different trades. These were called Craft Guilds, and the coats of arms on the right will show you the sort of crafts which were organised in this way.

Each guild was for the protection of its own people, naturally. They had their charities, as you saw on page 29, for helping widows and orphans, and often had a special chapel in one of the town churches, where a priest was paid to pray for members of the guild, both living and dead, but especially for the dead. The guildsmen did not forget that they had a duty to their customers, too. They believed that they were in business to make a living, but not to get as much as they could by hook or by crook.

The guilds tried to make sure that none of their members sold poor-quality goods. They only allowed men to set up in business as master craftsmen if they had been properly trained and tested. Any boy who wanted to learn a trade had to serve a long apprenticeship with a master, something like seven years, and during this time he would live in the master's house and shop. At the end of his time the apprentice would have to pass an examination set by the guild. Sometimes this involved making an article as well as he possibly could; such an article would be called the young man's 'master-piece', because if it was good enough he would be qualified to set up in business as a master craftsman. Usually the young man would not have enough money to begin a business of his own immediately, so he would take a job as a 'journeyman'. This word has nothing to do with travelling; it comes from the French 'journée', for a day's work. Journeymen and masters were all fully trained.

If a master sold poor-quality goods he would be punished, often by fines. If he went on doing it, the guild would expel him. This was a very serious punishment, because it would take away his livelihood. A guildsman could be punished also for charging too much, which was unfair to the customer; or for charging too little, which was an unfair way of taking trade away from other craftsmen.

Guild badges and arms, Florence:
1 Wine merchants
2 Carpenters
3 Furriers and Skinners

Zurich:
4 Tailors and Cutters
5 Fishermen and Boatmen

London:
6 Brewers

What was a fair price?
Enough to repay a man for his materials, time and skill, so that he earned enough to support his family.

The idea behind all this was that every man should make a reasonable living by working for it, and no more. The Church said so. Greed was wicked. It was particularly wrong to make money without working at all, such as by lending money at interest. This was called 'usury', and it was a sin. The Jews did it, but Christians believed that they were doomed to Hell anyway, because they were the people who denied and rejected Christ. If a Christian lent money, he ought to do it as an act of charity, and not expect to be repaid more than he had lent.

The guilds had a great respect for the Church. Besides the things you have already heard about, they used to have solemn processions on certain holy-days, and sometimes acted religious plays in the streets of the town. The famous York plays date from those days. Often a guild might be able to act some appropriate Bible story, such as Noah's Ark, for the guild of ship-carpenters. Because the old word for a craft or trade was 'mistery'—like the French word 'métier'—these plays were called 'mystery plays'. This might confuse anybody nowadays who did not know. A mystery play is simply a craft play.

Though all that they did shows us that the guilds must have been powerful, and loyally supported by their members, they did not prevent some men from becoming very rich indeed. One such craftsman, Richard Whittington, became Mayor of London in 1397. Remember, too, those rich men who helped to build churches. A merchant and an earl both helped to build Lavenham tower (page 10), and both wanted everybody to know of their generosity. Round the bottom of the tower are their marks; the star badge which the earl of Oxford's men had made famous on many a battlefield and, beside it, the trade mark which Thomas Spring put on his goods. That man had money, and he had pride.

A pageant, or mystery play staged on a cart. Every few years the old guild plays are still re-enacted in York.

Lavenham: the earl and the merchant.

Money wins

The rulers always thought that they needed more money than they had. Even in the early part of the Middle Ages, when lords and kings were paid in work, or food, or fighting men, money had often been needed. As time went on, many lords and kings preferred to take money instead of these things, because they found that with the money they could buy exactly what they wanted, instead of having to take what they were given. We saw, on page 59, how some lords were willing to accept money rents from their villeins, and this may often have been because they expected that they would get better work done by paying labourers to do it than by relying on somewhat unwilling serfs, who would take every opportunity of slacking and dodging. In very much the same way, kings sometimes preferred to take money from their vassals instead of knights. With this money, which was known as 'scutage' or 'shield-money' in England, a king could hire professional soldiers who would be probably more skilful than knights who spent most of their time looking after their manors. One of the reasons why so many barons hated King John of England was that he took scutage from them too often, and employed tough mercenaries who were quite willing to help the king against any barons who tried to revolt.

When great men, especially kings, could not get enough ready money any other way, they had to borrow it. The people who dealt in money, and could lend it, were the Jews, as you saw on page 78. Hated by most Christians, the Jews needed the protection of kings and lords, though this did not always save them from being robbed and murdered, and lords and kings did not always repay what they had been lent. But if there were risks in money-lending, there were also great profits to be made out of interest, and, in spite of the Church's disapproval of usury, Christians went into the business. Merchants from the cities of Italy became especially well known as money-lenders.

These men found an argument to meet the objections of the Church. They argued that they were taking great risks of losing their money when they lent it, and that they had to charge interest to repay themselves for bad debts; in the same way, a merchant was entitled to charge enough on his goods to guard against such disasters as shipwreck or robbery.

left:
Golden royal of King Charles IV of France, 1325.

left and right:
Golden ducat of King Sigismund of Hungary, who became Emperor in 1410. The shield shows the Hungarian arms quartered with the lion of Bohemia, which he also ruled.

right:
Golden ducat of Venice, about 1320. It shows the Doge, the elected head of the republic, kneeling before St Mark, the city's patron saint.

right:
Golden florin of Florence, thirteenth or fourteenth century, showing St John the Baptist.

Coins issued by kings and merchants (shown at twice actual size).

Whether it was because they were convinced by this argument, or whether they had to borrow money themselves and could not afford to be too strict, the leaders of the Church did not seem able to stand up for their old ideas. In the later Middle Ages Italian bankers were very important men.

Most business of this sort was done in coins of gold and silver. The value of the coin depended on the purity of the gold or silver of which it was made, and the weight. These were guaranteed by the people who issued the coin. As you saw, coins could be issued by cities or kings, and merchants soon got to know the best sorts. If a merchant could spot a forgery, and could tell if some of the precious metal had been scraped from the edges, and knew how much coins of one place were worth in the coinage of another, he could manage well enough. The great danger was robbery. Also, these coins were heavy and awkward to carry about, if a merchant had to deal with many.

Bankers, as the dealers in money were called, found a way of making it safer and easier. If a banker had one office, say, in Florence and another in Bruges, a man could pay money into the Bruges office and be given a piece of paper which allowed him to take the same amount out of the Florence office. After about the year 1300 many Italian banks had branches in the main cities of Europe; the main banking street of the city of London is still called Lombard Street. The Medici of Florence, from whose arms the three brass balls of the pawnbroker's sign may have originated, could, for instance, in the fifteenth century send letters to their branches or to their friends all over Europe, asking them to supply money to travellers or merchants, or lords or kings. By signing a piece of paper, a banker could be a valued friend or a dangerous opponent of any of the great rulers of Europe.

In this book you have seen the different classes or estates of men who lived during the Middle Ages. You have learned of the different sorts of people within those three great classes, and of the changes that happened in the Church, among the feudal ruling classes, and among the ordinary people—an enormous class, which included poor serfs and wealthy merchants. Among all the changes, it is possible that the growing power of money did most to upset the authority of the Church and the feudal lords.

The arms and badges of medieval princes have often continued and become emblems of present-day states. The Swedes still use the three crowns. When Edward III claimed to be King of France as well as England, he quartered the lilies of France on his shield with the leopards of England; the modern British royal standard unites the leopards with the lion of Scotland and the Irish harp. On her Communist flag Albania keeps the eagle of her medieval hero Scanderbeg. Many states use medieval badges on their coins, for example Belgium (1949), Portugal (1942), Austria (1960).

5. Kings and countries

We have been thinking of western Europe as a whole, because the most important things for us to understand about the Middle Ages were true all over western Europe. But it is also important to us that western Europe was divided into many parts. Different nations spoke different languages, and there were many kingdoms. This does not mean that each nation had a king of its own. Sometimes people of the same language, like the Spaniards, were divided into several kingdoms, and sometimes one king, like the king of France or England, ruled people who spoke several languages.

During the Middle Ages it happened in many countries that the people came to think of themselves more and more as members of a nation, and that the king made himself stronger while the Church and feudal lords lost power. You may have seen signs of this happening at various places in this book, and it becomes clearest if we look at the story of one or two kingdoms. Unfortunately there is no space in this book to tell the story of even one medieval kingdom, and of the great kings, bishops and lords who decided how it would grow. For the interesting details of the people and their actions you should read other books. On pages 84–91 there is instead a table, giving you an outline of what happened in one kingdom, England. This will let you fit together the things that happened to the three estates, and how they sometimes had an effect on one another. It also shows something we have not said much about, the way kings tried to get hold of other lands, which led to constant fighting.

Notice how the Church, after being very strong in the first part of the Middle Ages, especially in the reign of King John, lost power until by about 1400 it could not stand up to the king.

You will see that the feudal lords often caused trouble. Sometimes this helped other people as well as the barons themselves, as when Magna Carta was given, or when the king decided that country knights and townsmen were needed, as well as bishops and barons, to help and advise him in the great council which was called Parliament. Another very important thing to notice is how the lords came to rely less on their vassals when they went to war, and instead hired professional soldiers; and how they kept on such hired fighters in peacetime, calling them 'retainers' and dressing them in uniform called 'livery'. These were men who killed each other in large numbers during the Wars of the Roses, and so made it easier for a strong king, at the end, to make sure that the barons would never have another chance to keep gangs of armed men in their castles. In a way, the barons themselves were the people who destroyed the power of feudal lords.

The rise of the ordinary people can easily be seen. The peasants ceased to be serfs, and gained the respect of many a proud lord by their deadly skill with the longbow. The merchants were the people on whose money the king had to rely in order to make himself master of his kingdom.

A tremendous amount depended on what sort of a man the king was, and you can see that weak kings could lose their crowns and their lives. Strong kings often attacked their neighbours. You can see how the lands ruled by the king of England changed. One result of all the fighting seems to have been to make the people of England think of themselves more as being a special sort of people, the English nation, different from such people as Scots and French. English became the language of everybody in England, not only the common people, though it now contained French words which had been brought in by the nobles.

By the end of the Middle Ages the king of England was in a very strong position. The Church was past its best, and was more likely to need his help than to oppose him. The lords had been taught a severe lesson, and the feudal system did not work any longer. There was a Parliament, which allowed all the well-off people to help, and the king's courts kept law and order – feudal lords' courts and Church courts did not often try important cases. Most people in the country, as far as we can tell, were proud of being English, and liked having a strong king who made everybody obey him. England was becoming what is called a 'nation-state'.

England was not the only land where this sort of thing happened. As you can see from this map, there were many countries where the kings had become very powerful. In some lands the king was even stronger than the king of England, having a big army, which the king of England did not have, and being able to give orders to his Parliament much more than the king of England thought it safe to do. Even in the lands that had not turned into nation-states, like Italy and

Kings rise and fall as Fortune's wheel turns. This fourteenth-century English drawing illustrates the struggle for power in the medieval world.

Germany, there were often strong rulers who had built up small states in parts of the countries.

As you know, much of this had happened because the king was able to get money, and this was because the merchants had done well. This had happened in most lands, though there were many lands where the peasants had not done so well as in England, and still remained unfree. Almost everywhere, however, the other two estates had become too weak to resist the power of the king. Because the outstanding thing about the Middle Ages was the way the Church and the lords held power, we can see that the period called Middle Ages was ending.

From 1397 the crowns of
Norway, Denmark and Sweden
were united

FAROE IS. (N)

SHETLAND IS. (S)

K. OF NORWAY

K. OF SWEDEN

PR. OF MOSCOW

TEUTONIC KNIGHTS

K. OF SCOTLAND

K. OF
DENMARK

GRAND DUCHY
OF LITHUANIA

K. OF POLAND

From 1386 the crowns of
Poland and Lithuania
were united

IRELAND
(TO ENGLAND)

K. OF
ENGLAND

HOLY ROMAN EMPIRE

K. OF
BOHEMIA

From 1490 the crowns of
Bohemia and Hungary
were united

PR. OF
MOLDAVIA

SWISS
CONFEDERATION

D. OF
AUSTRIA

K. OF FRANCE

K. OF HUNGARY

From 1479 the crowns of Castile
and Aragon were united

D. OF SAVOY

D.
OF
MILAN

R. OF VENICE

R. OF GENOA

R. OF
FLORENCE

OTTOMAN

EMPIRE

K. OF
PORTUGAL

K. OF
ARAGON

CORSICA (G)

PAPAL
STATES

K. OF
NAPLES

K. OF CASTILE

BALEARIC IS. (A)

SARDINIA (A)

RHODES
(KTS OF
ST JOHN)

CYPRUS (V)

K. OF GRANADA
TO CASTILE 1492

SICILY (A)

CRETE (V)

To:
A   Aragon
G   Genoa
N   Norway
S   Scotland
V   Venice

0   100   200   300   400   500 miles

0   200   400   600   800 km

Lands held by Dukes of Burgundy before
the death of Charles the Bold 1477

The states of Europe in the later fifteenth century

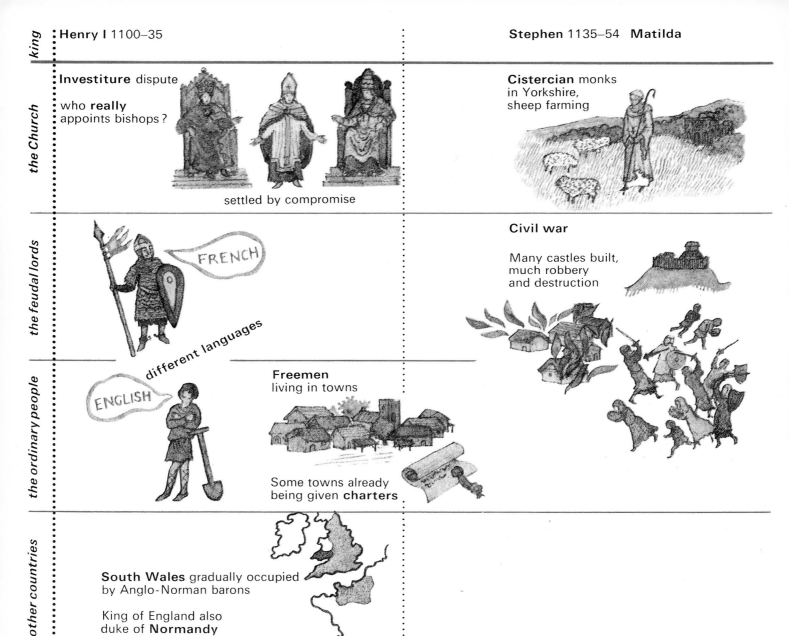

king

Henry I 1100–35

Stephen 1135–54 Matilda

the Church

Investiture dispute

who **really** appoints bishops?

settled by compromise

Cistercian monks in Yorkshire, sheep farming

the feudal lords

FRENCH

different languages

Civil war

Many castles built, much robbery and destruction

the ordinary people

ENGLISH

Freemen living in towns

Some towns already being given **charters**

other countries

South Wales gradually occupied by Anglo-Norman barons

King of England also duke of **Normandy**

AD 1100

1125

Henry II 1154–89

Richard I 1189–99

Quarrel about whether
king's courts could
try and punish **churchmen**

Murder of Archbishop Thomas Becket 1170

and severe **penance** of king

Firm government restored

The Third Crusade

Many castles pulled down

the feudal lords

Royal courts become strong e.g. **Assizes**

First **mayor**
of London 1189

the ordinary people

Ireland taken by barons
then by king of England

other countries

'**Angevin Empire**' Henry of **Anjou** became king
of England, married great heiress
Eleanor of **Aquitaine**

1150

1175

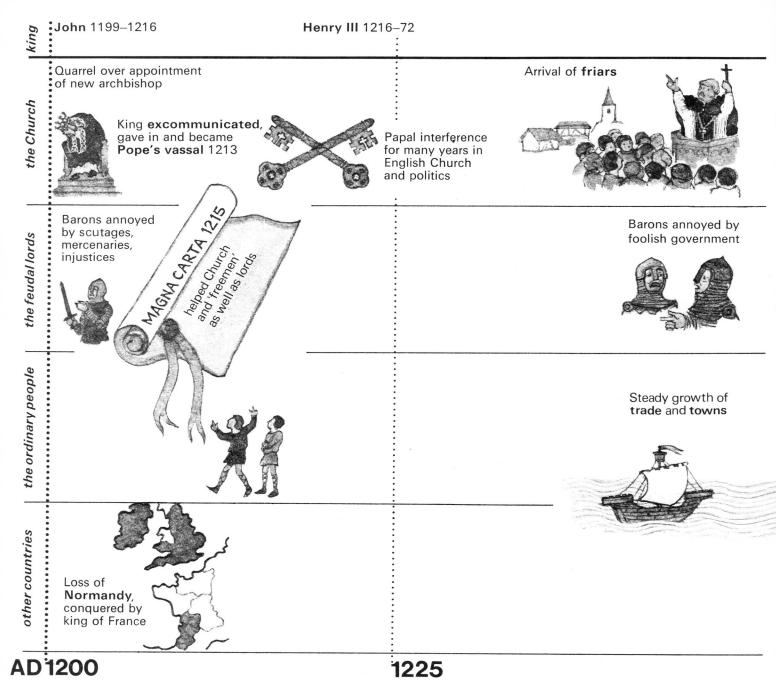

king
John 1199–1216　　　　　Henry III 1216–72

the Church
Quarrel over appointment of new archbishop

Arrival of **friars**

King **excommunicated**, gave in and became **Pope's vassal** 1213

Papal interference for many years in English Church and politics

the feudal lords
Barons annoyed by scutages, mercenaries, injustices

MAGNA CARTA 1215

helped Church and 'freemen' as well as lords

Barons annoyed by foolish government

the ordinary people
Steady growth of **trade** and **towns**

other countries
Loss of **Normandy**, conquered by king of France

AD 1200　　　　　　　1225

86

Edward I 1272–1307

Rise of **universities**

Law of **Mortmain** 1279
nobody allowed to give land to the Church
without king's permission

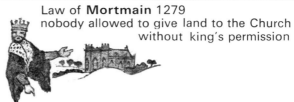

Gradual weakening of
papal power in England

Barons' War

De Montfort's Parliament 1265

including
country knights
and
townsmen

King decided that he
needed the help of
all his rich subjects
and began to hold this type of

*Bishops
and
barons*

HOUSE OF LORDS

PARLIAMENT

HOUSE OF
COMMONS
*Knights of shires
and
townsmen
of
boroughs*

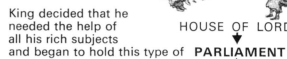

Attempt by king of England
to take **Scotland**

North Wales conducted by
king of England

1250   **1275**

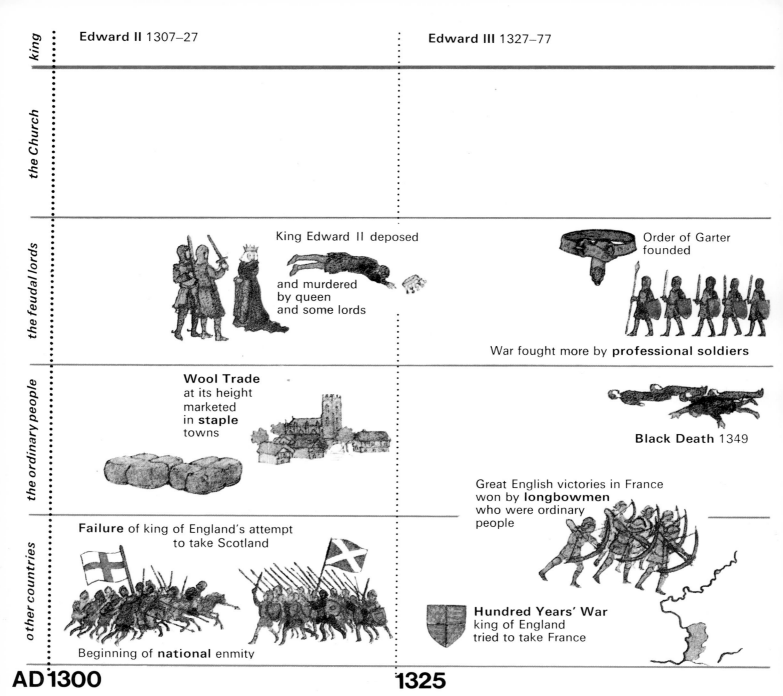

king

Edward II 1307–27   Edward III 1327–77

the Church

the feudal lords

King Edward II deposed

and murdered
by queen
and some lords

Order of Garter
founded

War fought more by **professional soldiers**

the ordinary people

Wool Trade
at its height
marketed
in **staple**
towns

Black Death 1349

Great English victories in France
won by **longbowmen**
who were ordinary
people

other countries

Failure of king of England's attempt
to take Scotland

Beginning of **national** enmity

Hundred Years' War
king of England
tried to take France

AD 1300   **1325**

Richard II 1377–99

Laws of **Provisors** and **Praemunire**
Pope's orders not to be obeyed
in England
unless king permitted

John Wyclif
began
Lollard heresy

the Church

less by feudal vassals

ENGLISH

King Richard II
deposed
and perhaps
murdered
by Henry
of Lancaster
and some
lords

the feudal lords

led to
shortage of
workmen –
demands for
higher wages

English language
now spoken by lords
as well as by
ordinary people

ENGLISH

Peasants' Revolt 1381 took London
but king's promises
to the peasants
were not kept

the ordinary people

King of England
took lands in
northern France

1360

French recovery
and truces

other countries

1350   **1375**

89

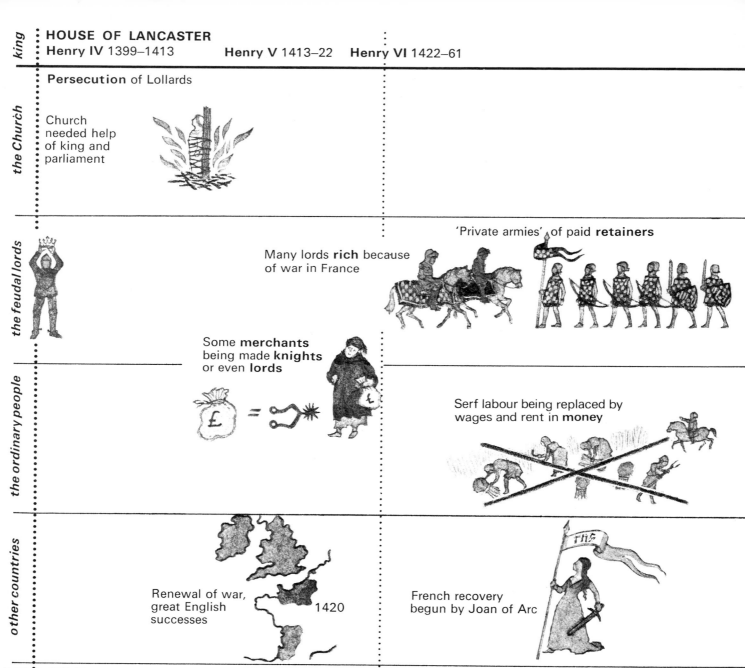

king	**HOUSE OF LANCASTER** Henry IV 1399–1413 Henry V 1413–22 Henry VI 1422–61

the Church

Persecution of Lollards

Church needed help of king and parliament

the feudal lords

Many lords **rich** because of war in France

'Private armies' of paid **retainers**

the ordinary people

Some **merchants** being made **knights** or even **lords**

£ = ⚙

Serf labour being replaced by wages and rent in **money**

other countries

Renewal of war, great English successes   1420

French recovery begun by Joan of Arc

AD 1400

1425

90

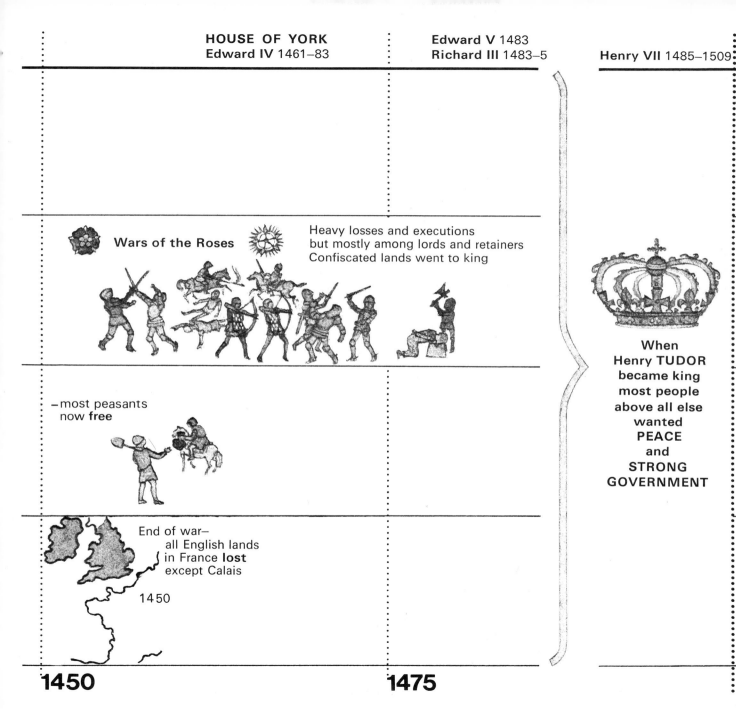

HOUSE OF YORK
Edward IV 1461–83

Edward V 1483
Richard III 1483–5

Henry VII 1485–1509

the Church

Wars of the Roses

Heavy losses and executions
but mostly among lords and retainers
Confiscated lands went to king

the feudal lords

When
Henry **TUDOR**
became king
most people
above all else
wanted
PEACE
and
**STRONG
GOVERNMENT**

—most peasants
now **free**

the ordinary people

End of war—
all English lands
in France **lost**
except Calais

1450

other countries

1450

1475

6. The end of the Middle Ages

A meeting of the Order of the Golden Fleece, 1473, shown on a contemporary manuscript.

A modern artist's reconstruction of the probable appearance of the Scottish spearmen whose hedgehog formation beat the English knights in the days of Robert Bruce.

The decline of the feudal lords

From what happened in England you can guess what happened in other lands of western Europe. Money upset the feudal idea. It bought mercenary soldiers, and it bought the expensive new guns. Guns seem to have been used for the first time in Europe about 1320, and were improved until they could knock the knights off their horses and pound holes in castle walls. This was bad enough, but even worse, from the feudal point of view, was the way that common people in many lands were showing that they could beat armoured knights without needing the help of gunpowder. You know about the longbow of the Welsh and the English. Other people were able to defeat knights, often with enormous slaughter, by using a variety of weapons. The Scots used long spears, the townsmen of Flanders long clubs, the Swiss halberds and pikes, the Bohemians war-flails and carts.

The lords and knights sensed what was happening, but did not want to admit it. Perhaps this is why so many orders of knighthood, like the Garter and the Golden Fleece, were founded in the later part of the Middle Ages, and why long tales about such heroes as the Knights of the Round Table were so very popular then. It all helped to make everyone feel that the lords and knights were still strong and important. They went on enjoying their wealth, and being regarded as the upper class, the nobility and gentry, better than the ordinary people; but no amount of make-believe could give them back the real power that they were losing.

A Bohemian waggon-fort of the 1420s, bristling with weapons: guns of different sizes, crossbows, a war-flail and a morning star, with one man apparently hurling a stone. The Hussite emblem of a chalice is on the tent, and the drawing is contemporary.

below: Flemish townsmen exclaimed 'Goedendag!' (Good-day) as they smote French knights at Courtrai, 1302, so their heavy clubs were called goedendags. Carving on a chest made at the time.

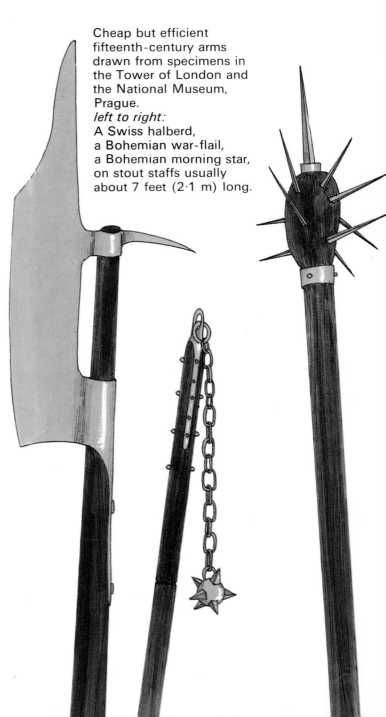

Cheap but efficient fifteenth-century arms drawn from specimens in the Tower of London and the National Museum, Prague.
left to right:
A Swiss halberd, a Bohemian war-flail, a Bohemian morning star, on stout staffs usually about 7 feet (2·1 m) long.

Chaucer's clergy, good and bad, from drawings in an early manuscript of *The Canterbury Tales*.
from left to right:
The Poor Parson: 'benign he was, and wondrous diligent'.
The Clerk of Oxford: 'gladly would he learn, and gladly teach'.
The Prioress: 'took pains to counterfeit the ways of court'.
The Monk: 'full many a dainty horse had he in stable'.
The Friar: 'he knew the taverns well in every town'.
The Summoner: 'of his visage children were afeared'.
The Pardoner: 'he had a pillow-case, which was, he said, Our Lady's veil'.

The decline of the medieval Church

The Church was also losing power. There was a little outright disbelief in some of the things that the Church taught. In England there were the Lollards who wanted to cut down the power and wealth of the Church and change some services. They had to be put down by the king. In Bohemia there were the followers of John Hus, whose ideas were rather like those of the Lollards, and the Hussites used their war-flails and battle-carts so well that at last the Church had to let them worship as they wished. This was the first time that a revolt against the Church had won. It was a dangerous sign.

More serious, though, was the way that people who still believed in all that the Church taught were losing their respect for the leaders of the Church. During most of the fourteenth century the Popes lived in Avignon, because the people of Rome had been too lawless and riotous for it to be safe there. Nowadays Avignon is inside France. Then it was just outside the French border, but many people thought that the Pope was under the thumb of the king of France. This was not very good for the Pope's reputation.

Worse was to follow. The Pope returned to Rome in 1378, and almost immediately there was an election for a new Pope, when the old one died. This election was disputed. Two men claimed to be Pope. Who was right? Churchmen could not agree. One Pope lived in Rome, the other in Avignon, and they hurled curses at each other. Kings had to make up their

minds which Pope their kingdoms would follow. It was an absurd situation for the 'one true undivided Church'. No doubt only one of the two was the real Head of the Church, but who could tell which?

At last a large number of the bishops and other leading churchmen from all parts of Europe began to hold councils. They failed at first, but in 1415 a council met at Constance, in southern Germany, and managed to get one man recognised by nearly everybody as the true Pope.

Even now things did not get back to normal. Many churchmen now thought that it would be safer if councils like that were to meet regularly, and that these councils would be entitled to tell the Pope what to do. It took the Popes another twenty years to defeat this threat to their authority.

While things were going wrong at the top, many churchmen lower down were losing the respect of the laymen. When the English poet Chaucer described all the different pilgrims in his *Canterbury Tales*, at the end of the fourteenth century, he showed very little respect for most churchmen. He thought that there were some good churchmen – and Chaucer himself believed firmly in the truth of what the Church taught – but that too many churchmen were just getting a comfortable life out of the Church, and that some of them were no better than liars and swindlers.

The Church was not earning the reverence and obedience that it had once been able to command.

ROME

Pope Pius II at Ancona, trying to assemble a crusading fleet. Painting by Pinturicchio forty years after.

The last Crusade

In the year 1453 the city of Constantinople was attacked once more by the Muslims. This time the attackers were a new Turkish people, the Ottoman Turks. The great Christian stronghold in the East was now in dire peril. The Pope called on the kings and princes, lords and knights of Christendom to march to the rescue, to take up their swords against the infidels once again, and go on the Crusade.

Not one of them stirred. Only the merchants of Genoa, who were afraid that they would lose their trading rights in Constantinople if the Turks took the city, sent help to the last Byzantine emperor.

For he was the last. Genoa alone could not do the work of all Western Christendom. Turkish guns smashed breaches in the mighty walls, the emperor died fighting, and the victorious Turks proudly placed upon their flags the crescent badge of Byzantium. The city was given a new name, Istanbul, and became the capital of the Turkish Empire.

In the Balkans and on the Mediterranean Sea, the power of the Turks increased. The Pope called for help, and none came. In 1464 Pope Pius II, worn out and heart-broken, died as he was about to sail himself, with no more than his own few ships, against the Turks.

The rulers of Europe had other business to attend to.

Index

Acknowledgments

Illustrations in this volume are reproduced by kind permission of the following:
Front cover, back cover, pp. 4 (reaper), 31, 59 (Luttrell Psalter), 79, Trustees of the British Museum; p. 4 (bishop), His Grace the Archbishop of Canterbury and the Trustees of the Lambeth Palace Library; pp. 4, 82, Lord Leicester, Dr W. O. Hassall and Educational Productions Ltd; pp. 6, 7, 8, 18 (lavatorium), 26 (St Cross), 32, 34, 38, 47, 56 (cruck cottage), 63, National Monuments Record Office; pp. 6 (Melbourne), 14 (ambulatory), Courtauld Institute of Art; p. 7 (Chipping Camden), Walter Scott Ltd; pp. 7 (Heckington), 69, A. F. Kersting; p. 8 (rood screen), David Campbell; pp. 9, 13, 24, 25, 96, Scala; pp. 10, 54, 59, Dr J. K. St Joseph and the Cambridge University Dept. of Aerial Photography; p. 12, Wim Swaan: *The Gothic Cathedral*, Paul Elek Productions Ltd; p. 13, T. Barucki; pp. 13 (Gerona), 14 (shrine), Foto Mas; p. 14 (choir), Perfecta Publications; p. 14, Verlag Druckerei Paderborn; p. 15, Mansell Collection; pp. 17, 22 (Mt Grace), 46, 55, 66, Aerofilms Ltd; pp. 20, 21, 57, 58, Department of the Environment (Crown copyright); p. 21 (cell), Alan Sorrell; p. 22, Charterhouse, London; p. 26, Chichester Photographic Service; p. 27, Bibliothèque Royale de Belgique; p. 28, B. E. Bettisen; p. 29, The Warburg Institute; pp. 30, 64, 65 (ewer), Victoria and Albert Museum; p. 33, Studio Maxwell; p. 34 (model), Saxon's Ltd; p. 35, Universitatsbibliothek Heidelberg; pp. 36–7, John Mollo/Hugh Evelyn Ltd; p. 38 (Rhine Castle), W. Heffer and Sons Ltd, Cambridge; p. 41, Louvre; p. 44, Les amis des Musées de Limoges; p. 45, BOAC; p. 49, Israel Government Tourist Office; p. 50, Librairie Hachette; pp. 54, 55 (plans), by courtesy of Thomas Sharp: *The Anatomy of the village*; p. 56 (thatching), British Tourist Authority; p. 56, Bord Failte Eireann; pp. 57 (utensils), 62, Trustees of the London Museum; p. 59 (reconstruction), Science Museum; pp. 60, 61, Giraudon; p. 64 (armour), Kunsthistorisches Museum Vienna; p. 65, Nicholas Servian/Woodmansterne Ltd; p. 69 (lantern tower), Turner's Ltd; p. 71, Kershaw Studios; p. 73, Italian State Tourist Office; p. 75, Foto Marburg; p. 75 (King's Lynn), Hallam Ashley; p. 78, York Evening Press; 79 (Lavenham tower marks), Captain G. A. D. Cooper; p. 92 (drawing), Don Pottinger; p. 92, Fitzwilliam Museum Cambridge; p. 93, Osterreichische Nationalbibliothek; p. 93 ('goedendags'), Thomas Photos, Oxford; pp. 94–5, Mary Evans Photo Library.

Paintings and drawings by Zena Flax
Maps by Peter Taylor
Diagrams by Banks and Miles

front cover: The Seal of Robert Fitz Walter (*Sigillum Roberti Filii Walteri*), a leader of the English barons against King John. Though only $2\frac{1}{4}$ inches (5·7 cm) high, it shows details very clearly.

back cover: Thomas Arundel, Archbishop of Canterbury, preaching for Henry of Lancaster against King Richard II. The original picture is $3\frac{1}{4}$ inches (8·2 cm) high, and comes from a French manuscript history written in the fifteenth century.

The Cambridge History Library

The Cambridge Introduction to History
Written by Trevor Cairns

PEOPLE BECOME CIVILIZED

THE ROMANS AND THEIR EMPIRE

BARBARIANS, CHRISTIANS, AND MUSLIMS

THE MIDDLE AGES

EUROPE AROUND THE WORLD

EUROPE AND THE WORLD

THE BIRTH OF MODERN EUROPE

THE OLD REGIME AND THE REVOLUTION

POWER FOR THE PEOPLE

The Cambridge Topic Books
General Editor Trevor Cairns

THE AMERICAN WAR OF INDEPENDENCE

BENIN: AN AFRICAN KINDGOM AND CULTURE

THE BUDDHA

BUILDING THE MEDIEVAL CATHEDRALS

CHRISTOPHER WREN
AND ST. PAUL'S CATHEDRAL

THE EARLIEST FARMERS AND THE FIRST CITIES

EARLY CHINA AND THE WALL

THE FIRST SHIPS AROUND THE WORLD

GANDHI AND THE STRUGGLE
FOR INDIA'S INDEPENDENCE

HERNAN CORTES: CONQUISTADOR IN MEXICO

THE INDUSTRIAL REVOLUTION BEGINS

LIFE IN A FIFTEENTH-CENTURY MONASTERY

LIFE IN A MEDIEVAL VILLAGE

LIFE IN THE IRON AGE

LIFE IN THE OLD STONE AGE

MARTIN LUTHER

MEIJI JAPAN

THE MURDER OF ARCHBISHOP THOMAS

MUSLIM SPAIN

THE NAVY THAT BEAT NAPOLEON

POMPEII

THE PYRAMIDS

THE ROMAN ARMY

THE ROMAN ENGINEERS

ST. PATRICK AND IRISH CHRISTIANITY

THE VIKING SHIPS

The Cambridge History Library will be expanded in the future to include additional volumes. Lerner Publications Company is pleased to participate in making this excellent series of books available to a wide audience of readers.

Lerner Publications Company
241 First Avenue North, Minneapolis, Minnesota 55401